D1505198

FIAT MONEY INFLATION
IN FRANCE

SPECIAL EDITION FOR
BANK OF NEW YORK & TRUST COMPANY
Established 1784

FIAT MONEY INFLATION IN FRANCE

How It Came, What It Brought, and How It Ended

BY

ANDREW DICKSON WHITE, LL.D., Ph.D., D.C.L.

Late President and Professor of History at Cornell University;
Sometime United States Minister to Russia and Am-
bassador to Germany; Author of ''A History of
the Warfare of Science with Theology,'' etc.

Mills College Library
Withdrawn

D. APPLETON-CENTURY COMPANY
INCORPORATED

NEW YORK   **LONDON**

1933

Copyright, 1896, by
D. APPLETON AND COMPANY

Copyright, 1923, by
MRS. ANDREW D. WHITE

All rights reserved. This book, or parts
thereof, must not be reproduced in any
form without permission of the publisher.

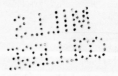

Printed in the United States of America

74733

332.5
W582f

INTRODUCTION

As far back as just before our Civil War I made, in France and elsewhere, a large collection of documents which had appeared during the French Revolution, including newspapers, reports, speeches, pamphlets, illustrative material of every sort, and, especially, specimens of nearly all the Revolutionary issues of paper money,—from notes of ten thousand *livres* to those of one *sou*.

Upon this material, mainly, was based a course of lectures then given to my students, first at the University of Michigan and later at Cornell University, and among these lectures, one on "Paper Money Inflation in France."

This was given simply because it showed one important line of facts in that great struggle; and I recall, as if it were yesterday, my feeling of regret at being obliged to bestow so much care and labor upon a subject to all appearance so utterly devoid of practical value. I am sure that it never occurred, either to my Michigan students or to myself, that it could ever have any bearing on our own country. It certainly never entered into our minds that any such folly as that exhibited in those French documents of the eighteenth century could ever find supporters in the United States of the nineteenth.

Some years later, when there began to be demands for large issues of paper money in the United States, I wrought some of the facts thus collected into a speech in the Senate of the State of New York, showing the need of especial care in such dealings with financial necessities.

In 1876, during the "greenback craze," General Garfield and Mr. S. B. Crittenden, both members of the House of Representatives at that time, asked me to read a paper on the same general subject before an audience of Senators and Representatives of both parties in Washington. This I did, and also gave it later before an assemblage of men of business at the Union League Club in New York.

Various editions of the paper were afterward published, among them, two or three for campaign purposes, in the hope that they might be of use in showing to what folly, cruelty, wrong and ruin the passion for "fiat money" may lead.

Other editions were issued at a later period, in view of the principle involved in the proposed unlimited coinage of silver in the United States, which was, at bottom, the idea which led to that fearful wreck of public and private prosperity in France.

For these editions there was an added reason in the fact that the utterances of sundry politicians at that time pointed clearly to issues of paper money practically unlimited. These men were logical enough to see that it would be inconsistent to stop at the unlimited issue of silver dollars which cost really something when they could issue unlimited paper dollars which virtually cost nothing.

In thus exhibiting facts which Bishop Butler would have recognized as confirming his theory of "The Possible Insanity of States," it is but just to acknowledge that the French proposal was vastly more sane than that made in our own country. Those French issues of paper rested not merely "on the will of a free people," but on one-third of the entire landed property of France; on the very choicest of real property in city and country—the confiscated estates of the Church and of the fugitive aristocracy—and on the power to use the paper thus issued in purchasing this real property at very low prices. * * *

I have taken all pains to be exact, revising the whole paper in the light of the most recent publications and giving my authority for every important statement, and now leave the whole matter with my readers.

At the request of a Canadian friend, who has expressed a strong wish that this work be brought down to date, I have again restudied the subject in the light of various works which have appeared since my earlier research,—

INTRODUCTION

especially Levasseur's "Histoire des classes ouvrières et de l'industrie en France,"—one of the really great books of the twentieth century;—Dewarmin's superb "Cent Ans de numismatique Française" and sundry special treatises. The result has been that large additions have been made regarding some important topics, and that various other parts of my earlier work have been made more clear by better arrangement and supplementary information.

ANDREW D. WHITE.

Cornell University,
September, 1912.

FOREWORD BY MR. JOHN MACKAY

I am greatly indebted to the generosity of Mr. Andrew D. White, the distinguished American scholar, author and diplomatist, for permission to print and to circulate privately a small edition of his exceedingly valuable account of the great currency-making experiment of the French Revolutionary Government. The work has been revised and considerably enlarged by Mr. White for the purpose of the present issue.

The story of "Fiat Money Inflation in France" is one of great interest to legislators, to economic students, and to all business and thinking men. It records the most gigantic attempt ever made in the history of the world by a government to create an inconvertible paper currency, and to maintain its circulation at various levels of value. It also records what is perhaps the greatest of all governmental efforts—with the possible exception of Diocletian's—to enact and enforce a legal limit of commodity prices. Every fetter that could hinder the will or thwart the wisdom of democracy had been shattered, and in consequence every device and expedient that untrammelled power and unrepressed optimism could conceive were brought to bear. But the attempts failed. They left behind them a legacy of moral and material desolation and woe, from which one of the most intellectual and spirited races of Europe has suffered for a century and a quarter, and will continue to suffer until the end of time. There are limitations to the powers of governments and of peoples that inhere in the constitution of things, and that neither despotisms nor democracies can overcome.

Legislatures are as powerless to abrogate moral and economic laws as they are to abrogate physical laws. They cannot convert wrong into right nor divorce effect from cause, either by parliamentary majorities, or by unity of supporting public opinion. The penalties of such legislative folly will always be exacted by inexorable time. While these propositions may be regarded as mere commonplaces, and while they are acknowledged in a general way, they are in effect denied by many of the legislative experiments and the tendencies of public opinion of the present day. The story, therefore, of the colossal folly of France in the closing part of the eighteenth century and its terrible fruits, is full of instruction for all men who think upon the problems of our own time.

From among an almost infinite variety, there are four great and fundamental facts that clearly emerge, namely,—

(1) Notwithstanding the fact that the paper currency issued was the direct obligation of the State, that much of it was interest bearing, and that all of it was secured upon the finest real estate in France, and that penalties in the way of fines, imprisonments and death were enacted from time to time to maintain its circulation at fixed values, there was a steady depreciation in value until it reached zero point and culminated in repudiation. The aggregate of the issues amounted to no less than the enormous and unthinkable sum of $9,500,000,-000, and in the middle of 1797 when public repudiation took place, there was no less than $4,200,000,000 in face value of assignats and mandats outstanding; the loss, as always, falling mostly upon the poor and the ignorant.

(2) In the attempt to maintain fixed values for the paper currency the Government became involved in an equally futile attempt to maintain a tariff of legal prices for commodities. Here again penalties of fines, of imprisonments and of death were powerless to accomplish the end in view.

(3) An wholesale demoralisation of society took place under which thrift, integrity, humanity, and every principle of morality were thrown into the welter of seething chaos and cruelty.

(4) The real estate upon which the paper currency was secured represented confiscations by the State of the lands of the Church and of the Emigrant Noblemen. These lands were appraised, according to Mr. White's narrative and other authorities, at $1,000,000,000. Here was

FOREWORD BY MR. JOHN MACKAY

a straight addition to the State's resources of $1,000,000,-000. It is ominously significant that within one hundred years under the "Peace of Frankfort" signed on the 10th May, 1871, the French nation agreed to pay a war indemnity to victorious Germany of exactly the same sum, namely, $1,000,000,000 in addition to the surrender of the province of Alsace and a considerable part of Lorraine. The great addition to the national wealth, therefore, effected by the immoral confiscation of the lands in question disappeared with compound territorial interest added under the visitation of relentless retribution.

Public opinion in our own country is so far sound on the question of currency, but signs are not lacking in some lay quarters of an inclination to sanction dangerous experiments. The doctrine of governmental regulation of prices, has, however, made its appearance in embryo. Class dissatisfaction is also on the increase. The confiscation of property rights under legal forms and processes is apt to be condoned when directed against unpopular interests and when limited to amounts that do not revolt the conscience. The wild and terrible expression given to these insidious principles in the havoc of the Revolution should be remembered by all. Nor should the fact be overlooked that, as Mr. White points out on Page 6, the National Assembly of France which originated and supported these measures contained in its membership the ablest Frenchmen of the day.

JOHN MACKAY.

Toronto General Trusts Building,
Toronto, 31st March, 1914.

FIAT MONEY INFLATION
IN FRANCE

HOW IT CAME, WHAT IT BROUGHT
AND HOW IT ENDED *

I.

EARLY in the year 1789 the French nation found itself in deep financial embarrassment: there was a heavy debt and a serious deficit.

The vast reforms of that period, though a lasting blessing politically, were a temporary evil financially. There was a general want of confidence in business circles; capital had shown its proverbial timidity by retiring out of sight as far as possible; throughout the land was stagnation.

Statesmanlike measures, careful watching and wise management would, doubtless, have ere long led to a return of confidence, a reappearance of money and a resumption of business; but these involved patience and self-denial, and, thus far in human history, these are the rarest products of political wisdom. Few nations have ever been able to exercise these virtues; and France was not then one of these few.†

There was a general search for some short road to prosperity: ere long the idea was set afloat that the great want of the country was more of the circulating medium; and

---

* A paper read before a meeting of Senators and Members of the House of Representatives of both political parties, at Washington, April 12th, and before the Union League Club, at New York, April 13th, 1876, and now (1914) revised and extended.

† For proof that the financial situation of France at that time was by no means hopeless, see Storch, "Economie Politique," vol. iv, p. 159.

this was speedily followed by calls for an issue of paper money. The Minister of Finance at this period was Necker. In financial ability he was acknowledged as among the great bankers of Europe, but his was something more than financial ability: he had a deep feeling of patriotism and a high sense of personal honor. The difficulties in his way were great, but he steadily endeavored to keep France faithful to those principles in monetary affairs which the general experience of modern times had found the only path to national safety. As difficulties arose the National Assembly drew away from him, and soon came among the members renewed suggestions of paper money: orators in public meetings, at the clubs and in the Assembly, proclaimed it a panacea—a way of "securing resources without paying interest." Journalists caught it up and displayed its beauties, among these men, Marat, who, in his newspaper, "The Friend of the People," also joined the cries against Necker, picturing him—a man of sterling honesty, who gave up health and fortune for the sake of France—as a wretch seeking only to enrich himself from the public purse.

Against this tendency toward the issue of irredeemable paper Necker contended as best he might. He knew well to what it always had led, even when surrounded by the most skillful guarantees. Among those who struggled to support ideas similar to his was Bergasse, a deputy from Lyons, whose pamphlets, then and later, against such issues exerted a wider influence, perhaps, than any others: parts of them seem fairly inspired. Any one to-day reading his prophecies of the evils sure to follow such a currency would certainly ascribe to him a miraculous foresight, were it not so clear that his prophetic power was due simply to a knowledge of natural laws revealed by history. But this current in favor of paper money became so strong that an effort was made to breast it by a compromise: and during the last months of 1789 and the first months of 1790 came discussions in the National Assembly looking to issues of notes based upon the landed property of the Church,—which was to be confiscated for that purpose. But care was to be taken; the issue was to be largely in the shape of notes of 1,000, 300 and 200 *livres*, too large to be used as ordinary currency, but of convenient size to be used in purchasing the Church lands; besides this, they were to bear interest and this would tempt holders to hoard them. The Assembly thus held back from issuing smaller obligations.

Remembrances of the ruin which had come from the great issues of smaller currency at an earlier day were still vivid. Yet the pressure toward a popular currency for universal use grew stronger and stronger. The finance committee of the Assembly reported that "the people demand a new circulating medium"; that "the circulation of paper money is the best of operations"; that "it is the most free because it reposes on the will of the people"; that "it will bind the interest of the citizens to the public good."

The report appealed to the patriotism of the French people with the following exhortation: "Let us show to Europe that we understand our own resources; let us immediately take the broad road to our liberation instead of dragging ourselves along the tortuous and obscure paths of fragmentary loans." It concluded by recommending an issue of paper money carefully guarded, to the full amount of four hundred million *livres*, and the argument was pursued until the objection to smaller notes faded from view. Typical in the debate on the whole subject, in its various phases, were the declarations of M. Matrineau. He was loud and long for paper money, his only fear being that the Committee had not authorized enough of it; he declared that business was stagnant, and that the sole cause was a want of more of the circulating medium; that paper money ought to be made a legal tender; that the Assembly should rise above prejudices which the failures of John Law's paper money had caused, several decades before. Like every supporter of irredeemable paper money then or since, he seemed to think that the laws of Nature had changed since previous disastrous issues. He said: "Paper money under a despotism is dangerous; it favors corruption; but in a nation constitutionally governed, which itself takes care in the emission of its notes, which determines their number and use, that danger no longer exists." He insisted that John Law's notes at first restored prosperity, but that the wretchedness and ruin they caused resulted from their overissue, and that such an overissue is possible only under a despotism.*

M. de la Rochefoucauld gave his opinion that "the *assignats* will draw specie out of the coffers where it is now hoarded.†

On the other hand, Cazalès and Maury showed that the result could only be disastrous. Never, perhaps, did a political prophecy meet with more exact fulfillment in every line than the terrible picture drawn in one of Cazalès' speeches in this debate. Still the current ran stronger and stronger; Petion made a brilliant oration in favor of the report, and Necker's influence and experience were gradually worn away.

Mingled with the financial argument was a strong political plea. The National Assembly had determined to confiscate the vast real property of the French Church,—the pious accumulations of fifteen hundred years. There were princely estates in the country, bishops' palaces and conventual buildings in the towns; these formed between one-fourth and one-third of the entire real property of France, and amounted in value to at least two thousand million *livres*. By a few sweeping strokes all this became the property of the nation. Never, apparently, did a government secure a more solid basis for a great financial future.‡

---

* See Moniteur, sitting of April 10, 1790.
† Ibid., sitting of April 15, 1790.
‡ For details of this struggle, see Buchez and Roux, "Histoire Parlementaire de la Révolution Française," vol. iii, pp. 364, 365, 404. For the wild utterances of Marat throughout this whole history, see the full set of his "L'ami du peuple" in the President White Collection of the Cornell University. For Bergasse's pamphlet and a mass of similar publications, see the same collection. For the effect produced by them, see Challamel, "Les Français sous la Révolution"; also De Goncourt, "La Société Française pendant la Révolution," &c. For the Report referred to, see Levasseur, "Histoire des classes ouvriès et de l'industrie en France de 1789 à 1870." Paris, 1903, vol. i., chap. 6. Levasseur (vol. 1, p. 120), a very strong conservative in such estimates, sets the total value of church property at two thousand millions; other authorities put it as high as twice that sum.

There were two special reasons why French statesmen desired speedily to sell these lands. First, a financial reason, —to obtain money to relieve the government. Secondly, a political reason,—to get this land distributed among the thrifty middle-classes, and so commit them to the Revolution and to the government which gave their title.

It was urged, then, that the issue of four hundred millions of paper, (not in the shape of interest-bearing bonds, as had at first been proposed, but in notes small as well as large), would give the treasury something to pay out immediately, and relieve the national necessities; that, having been put into circulation, this paper money would stimulate business; that it would give to all capitalists, large or small, the means for buying from the nation the ecclesiastical real estate, and that from the proceeds of this real estate the nation would pay its debts and also obtain new funds for new necessities: never was theory more seductive both to financiers and statesmen.

It would be a great mistake to suppose that the statesmen of France, or the French people, were ignorant of the dangers in issuing irredeemable paper money. No matter how skillfully the bright side of such a currency was exhibited, all thoughtful men in France remembered its dark side. They knew too well, from that ruinous experience, seventy years before, in John Law's time, the difficulties and dangers of a currency not well based and controlled. They had then learned how easy it is to issue it; how difficult it is to check its overissue; how seductively it leads to the absorption of the means of the workingmen and men of small fortunes; how heavily it falls on all those living on fixed incomes, salaries or wages; how securely it creates on the ruins of the prosperity of all men of meagre means a class of debauched speculators, the most injurious class that a nation can harbor,—more injurious, indeed, than pro-

---

See especially Taine, liv. ii, ch. I., who gives the valuation as "about four milliards." Sybel, "Gesch. der Revolutionszeit," gives it as two milliards and Briand, "La séparation," &c., agrees with him. See also De Nervo, "Finances Françaises," vol. ii, pp. 236-240; also Alison, "History of Europe," vol. i.

fessional criminals whom the law recognizes and can throttle; how it stimulates overproduction at first and leaves every industry flaccid afterward; how it breaks down thrift and develops political and social immorality. All this France had been thoroughly taught by experience. Many then living had felt the result of such an experiment—the issues of paper money under John Law, a man who to this day is acknowledged one of the most ingenious financiers the world has ever known; and there were then sitting in the National Assembly of France many who owed the poverty of their families to those issues of paper. Hardly a man in the country who had not heard those who issued it cursed as the authors of the most frightful catastrophe France had then experienced.*

It was no mere attempt at theatrical display, but a natural impulse, which led a thoughtful statesman, during the debate, to hold up a piece of that old paper money and to declare that it was stained with the blood and tears of their fathers.

And it would also be a mistake to suppose that the National Assembly, which discussed this matter, was composed of mere wild revolutionists; no inference could be more wide of the fact. Whatever may have been the character of the men who legislated for France afterward, no thoughtful student of history can deny, despite all the arguments and sneers of reactionary statesmen and historians, that few more keen-sighted legislative bodies have ever met than this first French Constitutional Assembly. In it were such men as Sieyès, Bailly, Necker, Mirabeau, Talleyrand, Du-Pont de Nemours and a multitude of others who, in various sciences and in the political world, had already shown

---

* For striking pictures of this feeling among the younger generation of Frenchmen, see Challamel, ''Sur la Révolution,'' p. 305. For general history of John Law's paper money, see Henri Martin, ''Histoire de France''; also Blanqui, ''Histoire de l'économie politique,'' vol. ii, pp. 65-87; also Senior on ''Paper Money,'' sec. iii, Pt. I, also Thiers, ''Histoire de Law''; also Levasseur, op. cit. Liv. i., chap. VI. Several specimens of John Law's paper currency are to be found in the White Collection in the Library of Cornell University,— some, numbered with enormous figures.

and were destined afterward to show themselves among the strongest and shrewdest men that Europe has yet seen.

But the current toward paper money had become irresistible. It was constantly urged, and with a great show of force, that if any nation could safely issue it, France was now that nation; that she was fully warned by her severe experience under John Law; that she was now a constitutional government, controlled by an enlightened, patriotic people,—not, as in the days of the former issues of paper money, an absolute monarchy controlled by politicians and adventurers; that she was able to secure every *livre* of her paper money by a virtual mortgage on a landed domain vastly greater in value than the entire issue; that, with men like Bailly, Mirabeau and Necker at her head, she could not commit the financial mistakes and crimes from which France had suffered under John Law, the Regent Duke of Orleans and Cardinal Dubois.

Oratory prevailed over science and experience. In April, 1790, came the final decree to issue four hundred millions of *livres* in paper money, based upon confiscated property of the Church for its security. The deliberations on this first decree and on the bill carrying it into effect were most interesting; prominent in the debate being Necker, Du Pont de Nemours, Maury, Cazalès, Petion, Bailly and many others hardly inferior. The discussions were certainly very able; no person can read them at length in the "Moniteur," nor even in the summaries of the parliamentary history, without feeling that various modern historians have done wretched injustice to those men who were then endeavoring to stand between France and ruin.

This sum—four hundred millions, so vast in those days— was issued in *assignats,* which were notes secured by a pledge of productive real estate and bearing interest to the holder at three per cent. No irredeemable currency has ever claimed a more scientific and practical guarantee for its goodness and for its proper action on public finances. On the one hand, it had what the world recognized as a most practical security,—a mortgage on productive real estate of vastly greater value than the issue. On the other hand, as the notes bore interest, there seemed cogent reason for their being withdrawn from circulation whenever they became redundant.*

As speedily as possible the notes were put into circulation. Unlike those issued in John Law's time, they were engraved in the best style of the art. To stimulate loyalty, the portrait of the king was placed in the center; to arouse public spirit, patriotic legends and emblems surrounded it; to stimulate public cupidity, the amount of interest which the note would yield each day to the holder was printed in the margin; and the whole was duly garnished with stamps and signatures to show that it was carefully registered and controlled.†

To crown its work the National Assembly, to explain the advantages of this new currency, issued an address to the French people. In this address it spoke of the nation as "delivered by this grand means from all uncertainty and from all ruinous results of the credit system." It foretold that this issue "would bring back into the public treasury, into commerce and into all branches of industry strength, abundance and prosperity." ‡

Some of the arguments in this address are worth recalling, and, among them, the following:— "Paper money is without inherent value unless it represents some special property. Without representing some special property it is inadmissible in trade to compete with a metallic currency, which has a value real and independent of the public action; therefore it is that the paper money which has only the public au-

---

* See Buchez and Roux, "Histoire Parlementaire," vol. v, p. 321, et seq. For an argument to prove that the *assignats* were, after all, not so well secured as John Law's money, see Storch, "Economie Politique," vol. iv, p. 160.

† For specimens of this first issue and of nearly every other issue during the French Revolution, see the extensive collection of originals in the Cornell University Library. For a 'virtually complete collection of photographic copies, see Dewamin, "Cent ans de numismatique française," vol. i, passim.

‡ See "Addresse de l'Assemblée nationale sur les emissions *d'assignats* monnaies," p. 5.

thority as its basis has always caused ruin where it has been established; that is the reason why the bank notes of 1720, issued by John Law, after having caused terrible evils, have left only frightful memories. Therefore it is that the National Assembly has not wished to expose you to this danger, but has given this new paper money not only a value derived from the national authority but a value real and immutable, a value which permits it to sustain advantageously a competition with the precious metals themselves." *

But the final declaration was, perhaps, the most interesting. It was as follows:—

"These *assignats,* bearing interest as they do, will soon be considered better than the coin now hoarded, and will bring it out again into circulation." The king was also induced to issue a proclamation recommending that his people receive this new money without objection.

All this caused great joy. Among the various utterances of this feeling was the letter of M. Sarot, directed to the editor of the Journal of the National Assembly, and scattered through France. M. Sarot is hardly able to contain himself as he anticipates the prosperity and glory that this issue of paper is to bring to his country. One thing only vexes him, and that is the pamphlet of M. Bergasse against the *assignats;* therefore it is after a long series of arguments and protestations, in order to give a final proof of his confidence in the paper money and his entire skepticism as to the evils predicted by Bergasse and others, M. Sarot solemnly lays his house, garden and furniture upon the altar of his country and offers to sell them for paper money alone.

There were, indeed, some gainsayers. These especially appeared among the clergy, who, naturally, abhorred the confiscation of Church property. Various ecclesiastics made speeches, some of them full of pithy and weighty arguments, against the proposed issue of paper, and there is

---

* Ibid., p. 10.

preserved a sermon from one priest theatening all persons
handling the new money with eternal damnation. But the
great majority of the French people, who had suffered
ecclesiastical oppression so long, regarded these utterances
as the wriggling of a fish on the hook, and enjoyed the sport
all the better.*

The first result of this issue was apparently all that the
most sanguine could desire: the treasury was at once greatly
relieved; a portion of the public debt was paid; creditors
were encouraged; credit revived; ordinary expenses were
met, and, a considerable part of this paper money having
thus been passed from the government into the hands of the
people, trade increased and all difficulties seemed to vanish.
The anxieties of Necker, the prophecies of Maury and Cazalès seemed proven utterly futile. And, indeed, it is quite
possible that, if the national authorities had stopped with
this issue, few of the financial evils which afterwards arose
would have been severely felt; the four hundred millions of
paper money then issued would have simply discharged the
function of a similar amount of specie. But soon there came
another result: times grew less easy; by the end of September, within five months after the issue of the four hundred millions in *assignats,* the government had spent them
and was again in distress.†

The old remedy immediately and naturally recurred to
the minds of men. Throughout the country began a cry for
another issue of paper; thoughtful men then began to recall
what their fathers had told them about the seductive path
of paper-money issues in John Law's time, and to remember
the prophecies that they themselves had heard in the debate on the first issue of *assignats* less than six months
before.

At that time the opponents of paper had prophesied that,
once on the downward path of inflation, the nation could not

---

* For Sarot, see ''Lettre de M. Sarot,'' Paris, April 19, 1790. As
to the sermon referred to see Levasseur as above, vol. i, p. 136.

† Von Sybel, ''History of the French Revolution,'' vol. i, p. 252;
also Levasseur, as above, pp. 137 and following.

be restrained and that more issues would follow. The supporters of the first issue had asserted that this was a calumny; that *the people* were now in control and that they could and would check these issues whenever they desired.

The condition of opinion in the Assembly was, therefore, chaotic: a few schemers and dreamers were loud and outspoken for paper money; many of the more shallow and easy-going were inclined to yield; the more thoughtful endeavored to breast the current.

One man there was who could have withstood the pressure: Mirabeau. He was the popular idol,—the great orator of the Assembly and much more than a great orator,—he had carried the nation through some of its worst dangers by a boldness almost godlike; in the various conflicts he had shown not only oratorical boldness, but amazing foresight. As to his real opinion on an irredeemable currency there can be no doubt. It was the opinion which all true statesmen have held, before his time and since,—in his own country, in England, in America, in every modern civilized nation. In his letter to Cerutti, written in January, 1789, hardly six months before, he had spoken of paper money as "A nursery of tyranny, corruption and delusion; a veritable debauch of authority in delirium." In one of his early speeches in the National Assembly he had called such money, when Anson covertly suggested its issue, "a loan to an armed robber," and said of it: "that infamous word, paper money, ought to be banished from our language." In his private letters written at this very time, which were revealed at a later period, he showed that he was fully aware of the dangers of inflation. But he yielded to the pressure: partly because he thought it important to sell the government lands rapidly to the people, and so develop speedily a large class of small landholders pledged to stand by the government which gave them their titles; partly, doubtless, from a love of immediate rather than of remote applause; and, generally, in a vague hope that the severe, inexorable laws of finance which had brought heavy punishments upon governments emitting an irredeemable currency in other lands, at other times, might in some way at this time, be warded off from France.*

The question was brought up by Montesquieu's report on the 27th of August, 1790. This report favored, with evident reluctance, an additional issue of paper. It went on to declare that the original issue of four hundred millions, though opposed at the beginning, had proved successful; that *assignats* were economical, though they had dangers; and, as a climax, came the declaration: "We must save the country." †

Upon this report Mirabeau then made one of his most powerful speeches. He confessed that he had at first feared the issue of *assignats,* but that he now dared urge it; that experience had shown the issue of paper money most serviceable; that the report proved the first issue of *assignats* a success; that public affairs had come out of distress; that ruin had been averted and credit established. He then argued that there was a difference between paper money of the recent issue and that from which the nation had suffered so much in John Law's time; he declared that the French nation had now become enlightened and he added, "Deceptive subtleties can no longer mislead patriots and men of sense in this matter." He then went on to say: "We must accomplish that which we have begun," and declared that there must be one more large issue of paper, guaranteed by the national lands and by the good faith of the French nation. To show how practical the system was he insisted that just as soon as paper money should become too abundant it would be absorbed in rapid purchases of national lands; and he made a very striking comparison between this self-adjusting, self-converting system and the rains descending in showers upon the earth, then in swelling rivers discharged into the sea, then drawn up in vapor and finally scattered over the earth again in rapidly fertilizing showers.

* For Mirabeau's real opinion on irredeemable paper, see his letter to Cerutti, in a leading article of the ''Moniteur''; also ''Mèmoires de Mirabeau,'' vol. vii, pp. 23, 24 and elsewhere. For his pungent remarks above quoted, see Levasseur, ibid., vol. i, p. 118.

† See ''Moniteur,'' August 27, 1790.

He predicted that the members would be surprised at the astonishing success of this paper money and that there would be none too much of it.

His theory grew by what it fed upon,—as the paper-money theory has generally done. Toward the close, in a burst of eloquence, he suggested that *assignats* be created to an amount sufficient to cover the national debt, and that all the national lands be exposed for sale immediately, predicting that thus prosperity would return to the nation and that all classes would find this additional issue of paper money a blessing.*

This speech was frequently interrupted by applause; a unanimous vote ordered it printed, and copies were spread throughout France. The impulse given by it permeated all subsequent discussion; Gouy arose and proposed to liquidate the national debt of twenty-four hundred millions,—to use his own words—"by one single operation, grand, simple, magnificent." † This "operation" was to be the emission of twenty-four hundred millions in legal tender notes, and a law that specie should not be accepted in purchasing national lands. His demagogy bloomed forth magnificently. He advocated an appeal to the people, who, to use his flattering expression, "ought alone to give the law in a matter so interesting." The newspapers of the period, in reporting his speech, noted it with the very significant remark, "This discourse was loudly applauded."

To him replied Brillat-Savarin. He called attention to the depreciation of *assignats* already felt. He tried to make the Assembly see that natural laws work as inexorably in France as elsewhere; he predicted that if this new issue were made there would come a depreciation of thirty per cent. Singular, that the man who so fearlessly stood against this tide of unreason has left to the world simply a reputation as the most brilliant cook that ever existed! He was fol-

---

* "Moniteur," August 28, 1790; also Levasseur, as above, pp. 139 *et seq.*
† "Par une seule opération, grande, simple, magnifique." See "Moniteur." The whole sounds curiously like the proposals of the "Greenbackers," regarding the American debt, some years since.

lowed by the Abbe Goutes, who declared,—what seems grotesque to those who have read the history of an irredeemable paper currency in any country—that new issues of paper money "will supply a circulating medium which will protect public morals from corruption." *

Into this debate was brought a report by Necker. He was not, indeed, the great statesman whom France especially needed at this time, of all times. He did not recognize the fact that the nation was entering a great revolution, but he could and did see that, come what might, there were simple principles of finance which must be adhered to. Most earnestly, therefore, he endeavored to dissuade the Assembly from the proposed issue; suggesting that other means could be found for accomplishing the result, and he predicted terrible evils. But the current was running too fast. The only result was that Necker was spurned as a man of the past; he sent in his resignation and left France forever.† The paper-money demagogues shouted for joy at his departure; their chorus rang through the journalism of the time. No words could express their contempt for a man who was unable to see the advantages of filling the treasury with the issues of a printing press. Marat, Hébert, Camille Desmoulins and the whole mass of demagogues so soon to follow them to the guillotine were especially jubilant.‡

Continuing the debate, Rewbell attacked Necker, saying that the *assignats* were not at par because there were not yet enough of them; he insisted that payments for public lands be received in *assignats* alone; and suggested that the church bells of the kingdom be melted down into small money. Le Brun attacked the whole scheme in the Assembly, as he had done in the Committee, declaring that the proposal, instead of relieving the nation, would wreck it. The papers of the time very significantly say that at this there arose many murmurs. Chabroud came to the rescue. He

---

* "Moniteur," August 29, 1790.
† See Lacretelle, "18me Siécle," vol. viii, pp. 84-87; also Thiers and Mignet.
‡ See Hatin, "Histoire de la Presse en France," vols. v and vi.

said that the issue of *assignats* would relieve the distress of the people and he presented very neatly the new theory of paper money and its basis in the following words: "The earth is the source of value; you cannot distribute the earth in a circulating value, but this paper becomes representative of that value and it is evident that the creditors of the nation will not be injured by taking it." On the other hand, appeared in the leading paper, the "Moniteur," a very thoughtful article against paper money, which sums up all by saying, "It is, then, evident that all paper which cannot, at the will of the bearer, be converted into specie cannot discharge the functions of money." This article goes on to cite Mirabeau's former opinion in his letter to Cerutti, published in 1789,—the famous opinion of paper money as "a nursery of tyranny, corruption and delusion; a veritable debauch of authority in delirium." Lablache, in the Assembly, quoted a saying that "paper money is the emetic of great states." *

Boutidoux, resorting to phrasemaking, called the assignats *"un papier terre,"* or "land converted into paper." Boislandry answered vigorously and foretold evil results. Pamphlets continued to be issued,—among them, one so pungent that it was brought into the Assembly and read there,—the truth which it presented with great clearness being simply that doubling the quantity of money or substitutes for money in a nation simply increases prices, disturbs values, alarms capital, diminishes legitimate enterprise, and so decreases the demand both for products and for labor; that the only persons to be helped by it are the rich who have large debts to pay. This pamphlet was signed "A Friend of the People," and was received with great applause by the thoughtful minority in the Assembly. Du Pont de Nemours, who had stood by Necker in the debate on the first issue of *assignats,* arose, avowed the pamphlet to be his, and said sturdily that he had always voted against the emission of irredeemable paper and always would.†

---

* See ''Moniteur,'' Sept. 5, 6 and 20, 1790.
† See Levasseur, vol. i, p. 142.

Far more important than any other argument against inflation was the speech of Talleyrand. He had been among the boldest and most radical French statesmen. He it was,— a former bishop,—who, more than any other, had carried the extreme measure of taking into the possession of the nation the great landed estates of the Church, and he had supported the first issue of four hundred millions. But he now adopted a judicial tone—attempted to show to the Assembly the very simple truth that the effect of a second issue of *assignats* may be different from that of the first; that the first was evidently needed; that the second may be as injurious as the first was useful. He exhibited various weak points in the inflation fallacies and presented forcibly the trite truth that no laws and no decrees can keep large issues of irredeemable paper at par with specie.

In his speech occur these words: "You can, indeed, arrange it so that the people shall be forced to take a thousand *livres* in paper for a thousand *livres* in specie; but you can never arrange it so that a man shall be obliged to give a thousand *livres* in specie for a thousand *livres* in paper,— in that fact is embedded the entire question; and on account of that fact the whole system fails." *

The nation at large now began to take part in the debate; thoughtful men saw that here was the turning point between good and evil; that the nation stood at the parting of the ways. Most of the great commercial cities bestirred themselves and sent up remonstrances against the new emission,—twenty-five being opposed and seven in favor of it.

But eloquent theorists arose to glorify paper and among these, Royer, who on September 14, 1790, put forth a pamphlet entitled "Reflections of a Patriotic Citizen on the Issue of *Assignats*," in which he gave many specious reasons why the *assignats* could not be depressed, and spoke of the argument against them as "vile clamors of people bribed to affect public opinion." He said to the National Assembly,

---

* See speech in ''Moniteur''; also in Appendix to Thiers' ''History of the French Revolution.''

"If it is necessary to create five thousand millions, and more, of the paper, decree such a creation gladly." He, too, predicted, as many others had done, a time when gold was to lose all its value, since all exchanges would be made with this admirable, guaranteed paper, and therefore that coin would come out from the places where it was hoarded. He foretold prosperous times to France in case these great issues of paper were continued and declared these "the only means to insure happiness, glory and liberty to the French nation." Speeches like this gave courage to a new swarm of theorists,—it began to be especially noted that men who had never shown any ability to make or increase fortunes for themselves abounded in brilliant plans for creating and increasing wealth for the country at large.

Greatest force of all, on September 27, 1790, came Mirabeau's final speech. The most sober and conservative of his modern opponents speaks of its eloquence as "prodigious." In this the great orator dwelt first on the political necessity involved, declaring that the most pressing need was to get the government lands into the hands of the people, and so to commit to the nation and against the old privileged classes the class of landholders thus created.

Through the whole course of his arguments there is one leading point enforced with all his eloquence and ingenuity —the excellence of the proposed currency, its stability and its security. He declares that, being based on the pledge of public lands and convertible into them, the notes are better secured than if redeemable in specie; that the precious metals are only employed in the secondary arts, while the French paper money represents the first and most real of all property, the source of all production, *the land;* that while other nations have been obliged to emit paper money, none have ever been so fortunate as the French nation, for the reason that none had ever before been able to give this landed security; that whoever takes French paper money has practically a mortgage to secure it,—and on landed property which can easily be sold to satisfy his claims, while other nations have been able only to give a vague claim on the entire nation. "And," he cries, "I would rather have a mortgage on a garden than on a kingdom!"

Other arguments of his are more demagogical. He declares that the only interests affected will be those of bankers and capitalists, but that manufacturers will see prosperity restored to them. Some of his arguments seem almost puerile, as when he says, "If gold has been hoarded through timidity or malignity, the issue of paper will show that gold is not necessary, and it will then come forth." But, as a whole, the speech was brilliant; it was often interrupted by applause; it settled the question. People did not stop to consider that it was the dashing speech of an orator and not the matured judgment of a financial expert; they did not see that calling Mirabeau or Talleyrand to advise upon a monetary policy, because they had shown boldness in danger and strength in conflict, was like summoning a prize-fighter to mend a watch.

In vain did Maury show that, while the first issues of John Law's paper had brought prosperity, those that followed brought misery; in vain did he quote from a book published in John Law's time, showing that Law was at first considered a patriot and friend of humanity; in vain did he hold up to the Assembly one of Law's bills and appeal to their memories of the wretchedness brought upon France by them; in vain did Du Pont present a simple and really wise plan of substituting notes in the payment of the floating debt which should not form a part of the ordinary circulating medium; nothing could resist the eloquence of Mirabeau. Barnave, following, insisted that "Law's paper was based upon the phantoms of the Mississippi; ours, upon the solid basis of ecclesiastical lands," and he proved that the *assignats* could not depreciate further. Prudhomme's newspaper poured contempt over gold as security for the currency, extolled real estate as the only true basis and was fervent in praise of the convertibility and self-adjusting features of the proposed scheme. In spite of all this plausibility and eloquence, a large minority stood firm to their earlier principles; but on the 29th of September, 1790, by a vote of 508 to 423, the deed was done; a bill was passed authorizing the issue of eight hundred millions of new *assignats,* but solemnly declaring that in no case should the entire amount put in circulation exceed twelve hundred millions. To make assurance doubly sure, it also provided that as fast as the *assignats* were paid into the treasury for land they should be burned, and thus a healthful contraction be constantly maintained. Unlike the first issue, these new notes were to bear no interest.*

Great were the plaudits of the nation at this relief. Among the multitudes of pamphlets expressing this joy which have come down to us the "Friend of the Revolution" is the most interesting. It begins as follows: "Citizens, the deed is done. The *assignats* are the keystone of the arch. It has just been happily put in position. Now I can announce to you that the Revolution is finished and there only remain one or two important questions. All the rest is but a matter of detail which cannot deprive us any longer of the pleasure of admiring this important work in its entirety. The provinces and the commercial cities which were at first alarmed at the proposal to issue so much paper money now send expressions of their thanks; specie is coming out to be joined with paper money. Foreigners come to us from all parts of Europe to seek their happiness under laws which they admire; and soon France, enriched by her new property and by the national industry which is preparing for fruitfulness, will demand still another creation of paper money."

France was now fully committed to a policy of inflation; and, if there had been any question of this before, all doubts were removed now by various acts very significant as showing the exceeding difficulty of stopping a nation once in the full tide of a depreciating currency. The National Assembly had from the first shown an amazing liberality to all sorts of enterprises, wise or foolish, which were urged "for the good of the people." As a result of these and other largesses the old cry of the "lack of a circulating medium" broke

---

* See Levasseur, "Classes ouvrières," etc., vol. i, p. 149.

forth again; and especially loud were the clamors for more small bills. The cheaper currency had largely driven out the dearer; paper had caused small silver and copper money mainly to disappear; all sorts of notes of hand, circulating under the name of "confidence bills," flooded France,— sixty-three kinds in Paris alone. This unguaranteed currency caused endless confusion and fraud. Different districts of France began to issue their own *assignats* in small denominations, and this action stirred the National Assembly to evade the solemn pledge that the circulation should not go above twelve hundred millions and that all *assignats* returned to the treasury for lands should immediately be burned.* Within a short time there had been received into the treasury for lands one hundred and sixty million *livres* in paper. By the terms of the previous acts this amount of paper ought to have been retired. Instead of this, under the plea of necessity, the greater part of it was reissued in the form of small notes.

There was, indeed, much excuse for new issues of small notes, for, under the theory that an issue of smaller notes would drive silver out of circulation, the smallest authorized *assignat* was for fifty *livres*. To supply silver and copper and hold it in circulation everything was tried. Citizens had been spurred on by law to send their silverware and jewels to the mint. Even the king sent his silver and gold plate, and the churches and convents were required by law to send to the government melting pot all silver and gold vessels not absolutely necessary for public worship. For copper money the church bells were melted down. But silver and even copper continued to become more and more scarce. In the midst of all this, various juggleries were tried, and in November, 1790, the Assembly decreed a single standard of coinage, the chosen metal being silver, and the ratio between the two precious metals was changed from $15\frac{1}{2}$ to 1, to $14\frac{1}{2}$ to 1,—but all in vain. It was found necessary to issue the dreaded small paper, and a beginning was made by issu-

---

* See Levasseur, pp. 151 et seq. Various examples of these "confidence bills" are to be seen in the Library of Cornell University.

ing one hundred millions in notes of five *francs*, and, ere long, obedient to the universal clamor, there were issued parchment notes for various small amounts down to a single *sou*.*

Yet each of these issues, great or small, was but as a drop of cold water to a parched throat. Although there was already a rise in prices which showed that the amount needed for circulation had been exceeded, the cry for "more circulating medium" was continued. The pressure for new issues became stronger and stronger. The Parisian populace and the Jacobin Club were especially loud in their demands for them; and, a few months later, on June 19, 1791, with few speeches, in a silence very ominous, a new issue was made of six hundred millions more;—less than nine months after the former great issue, with its solemn pledges to keep down the amount in circulation. With the exception of a few thoughtful men, the whole nation again sang paeans.†

In this comparative ease of new issues is seen the action of a law in finance as certain as the working of a similar law in natural philosophy. If a material body fall from a height its velocity is accelerated, by a well-known law, in a constantly increasing ratio: so in issues of irredeemable currency, in obedience to the theories of a legislative body or of the people at large, there is a natural law of rapidly increasing emission and depreciation. The first inflation bills were passed with great difficulty, after very sturdy resistance and by a majority of a few score out of nearly a thousand votes; but we observe now that new inflation measures were passed more and more easily and we shall have occasion to see the working of this same law in a more striking degree as this history develops itself.

During the various stages of this debate there cropped up a doctrine old and ominous. It was the same which appeared toward the end of the nineteenth century in the United States during what became known as the "greenback

---

* See Levasseur, vol. i, pp. 155-156.
† See Von Sybel, ''History of the Revolution,'' vol. i, p. 265; also Levasseur, as above, vol. i, pp. 152-160.

craze" and the free "silver craze." In France it had been refuted, a generation before the Revolution, by Turgot, just as brilliantly as it was met a hundred years later in the United States by James A. Garfield and his compeers. This was the doctrine that all currency, whether gold, paper, leather or any other material, derives its efficiency from the official stamp it bears, and that, this being the case, a government may relieve itself of its debts and make itself rich and properous simply by means of a printing press:— fundamentally the theory which underlay the later American doctrine of "fiat money."

There came mutterings and finally speeches in the Jacobin Club, in the Assembly and in newspaper articles and pamphlets throughout the country, taking this doctrine for granted. These could hardly affect thinking men who bore in mind the calamities brought upon the whole people, and especially upon the poorer classes, by this same theory as put in practice by John Law, or as refuted by Turgot, but it served to swell the popular chorus in favor of the issue of more *assignats* and plenty of them.*

The great majority of Frenchmen now became desperate optimists, declaring that inflation is prosperity. Throughout France there came temporary good feeling. The nation was becoming inebriated with paper money. The good feeling was that of a drunkard just after his draught; and it is to be noted as a simple historical fact, corresponding to a physiological fact, that, as draughts of paper money came faster the successive periods of good feeling grew shorter.

Various bad signs began to appear. Immediately after each new issue came a marked depreciation; curious it is to note the general reluctance to assign the right reason. The decline in the purchasing power of paper money was in obedience to the simplest laws in economics, but France had now gone beyond her thoughtful statesmen and taken refuge in unwavering optimism, giving any explanation of the new

---

* For Turgot's argument against "fiat money" theory, see A. D. White, "Seven Great Statesmen in the Warfare of Humanity with Unreason," article on Turgot, pp. 169, et seq.

difficulties rather than the right one. A leading member of the Assembly insisted, in an elaborate speech, that the cause of depreciation was simply the want of knowledge and of confidence among the rural population and he suggested means of enlightening them. La Rochefoucauld proposed to issue an address to the people showing the goodness of the currency and the absurdity of preferring coin. The address was unanimously voted. As well might they have attempted to show that a beverage made by mixing a quart of wine and two quarts of water would possess all the exhilarating quality of the original, undiluted liquid.

Attention was aroused by another menacing fact;—specie disappeared more and more. The explanations of this fact also displayed wonderful ingenuity in finding false reasons and in evading the true one. A very common explanation was indicated in Prudhomme's newspaper, "Les Révolutions de Paris," of January 17, 1791, which declared that coin "will keep rising until the people shall have hanged a broker." Another popular theory was that the Bourbon family were, in some mysterious way, drawing off all solid money to the chief centers of their intrigues in Germany. Comic and, at the same time, pathetic, were evidences of the wide-spread idea that if only a goodly number of people engaged in trade were hanged, the par value of the *assignats* would be restored.

Still another favorite idea was that British emissaries were in the midst of the people, instilling notions hostile to paper. Great efforts were made to find these emissaries and more than one innocent person experienced the popular wrath under the supposition that he was engaged in raising gold and depressing paper. Even Talleyrand, shrewd as he was, insisted that the cause was simply that the imports were too great and the exports too little.* As well might he

---

* See De Goncourt, "Société française," for other explanations; "Les Révolutions de Paris," vol. ii, p. 216; Challamel, "Les Français sous la Révolution"; Senior, "On Some Effects of Paper Money," p. 82; Buchez and Roux, "Histoire Parlementaire," etc., vol. x, p. 216; Aulard, "Paris pendant la Révolution thermidorienne," *passim*, and especially "Rapport du bureau de surveillance," vol. ii, pp. 562, et seq. (Dec. 4-24, 1795.)

explain that fact that, when oil is mingled with water, water sinks to the bottom, by saying that this is because the oil rises to the top. This disappearance of specie was the result of a natural law as simple and as sure in its action as gravitation; the superior currency had been withdrawn because an inferior currency could be used.* Some efforts were made to remedy this. In the municipality of Quilleboeuf a considerable amount in specie having been found in the possession of a citizen, the money was seized and sent to the Assembly. The people of that town treated this hoarded gold as the result of unpatriotic wickedness or madness, instead of seeing that it was but the sure result of a law working in every land and time, when certain causes are present. Marat followed out this theory by asserting that death was the proper penalty for persons who thus hid their money.

Still another troublesome fact began now to appear. Though paper money had increased in amount, prosperity had steadily diminished. In spite of all the paper issues, commercial activity grew more and more spasmodic. Enterprise was chilled and business became more and more stagnant. Mirabeau, in his speech which decided the second great issue of paper, had insisted that, though bankers might suffer, this issue would be of great service to manufacturers and restore prosperity to them and their workmen. The latter were for a time deluded, but were at last rudely awakened from this delusion. The plenty of currency had at first stimulated production and created a great activity in manufactures, but soon the markets were glutted and the demand was diminished. In spite of the wretched financial policy of years gone by, and especially in spite of the Revocation of the Edict of Nantes, by which religious bigotry had driven out of the kingdom thousands of its most skillful Protestant workmen, the manufactures of France had before the Revolution come into full bloom. In the finer woolen goods, in

---

* For statements and illustration of the general action of this law, see Sumner, ''History of American Currency,'' pp. 157, 158; also Jevons, on ''Money,'' p. 80.

silk and satin fabrics of all sorts, in choice pottery and por-
celain, in manufactures of iron, steel, and copper, they had
again taken their old leading place upon the Continent. All
the previous changes had, at the worst, done no more than
to inflict a momentary check on this highly developed system
of manufactures. But what the bigotry of Louis XIV and the
shiftlessness of Louis XV could not do in nearly a century,
was accomplished by this tampering with the currency in
a few months. One manufactory after another stopped. At
one town, Lodève, five thousand workmen were discharged
from the cloth manufactories. Every cause except the right
one was assigned for this. Heavy duties were put upon
foreign goods; everything that tariffs and custom-houses
could do was done. Still the great manufactories of Nor-
mandy were closed, those of the rest of the kingdom speedily
followed, and vast numbers of workmen in all parts of the
country were thrown out of employment.* Nor was this the
case with the home demand alone. The foreign demand
which at first had been stimulated, soon fell off. In no way
can this be better stated than by one of the most thoughtful historians of modern times, who says, "It is true that
at first the *assignats* gave the same impulse to business in
the city as in the country, but the apparent improvement
had no firm foundation, even in the towns. Whenever a great
quantity of paper money is suddenly issued we invariably
see a rapid increase of trade. The great quantity of the
circulating medium sets in motion all the energies of commerce and manufactures; capital for investment is more
easily found than usual and trade perpetually receives
fresh nutriment. If this paper represents real credit, founded
upon order and legal security, from which it can derive
a firm and lasting value, such a movement may be the start-
ing point of a great and widely-extended prosperity, as, for
instance, a splendid improvement in English agriculture was
undoubtedly owing to the emancipation of the country bankers. If on the contrary, the new paper is of precarious value,
as was clearly seen to be the case with the French *assignats*

---

* See De Goncourt, "Société Française," p. 214.

as early as February, 1791, it can confer no lasting benefits. For the moment, perhaps, business receives an impulse, all the more violent because every one endeavors to invest his doubtful paper in buildings, machines and goods, which, under all circumstances, retain some intrinsic value. Such a movement was witnessed in France in 1791, and from every quarter there came satisfactory reports of the activity of manufactures."

"But, for the moment, the French manufacturers derived great advantage from this state of things. As their products could be so cheaply paid for, orders poured in from foreign countries to such a degree that it was often difficult for the manufacturers to satisfy their customers. It is easy to see that prosperity of this kind must very soon find its limit. ... When a further fall in the *assignats* took place this prosperity would necessarily collapse, and be succeeded by a crisis all the more destructive the more deeply men had engaged in speculation under the influence of the first favorable prospects." *

Thus came a collapse in manufacturing and commerce, just as it had come previously in France: just as it came at various periods in Austria, Russia, America, and in all countries where men have tried to build up prosperity on irredeemable paper.†

All this breaking down of the manufactures and commerce of the nation made fearful inroads on the greater fortunes; but upon the lesser, and upon the little properties of the masses of the nation who relied upon their labor, it pressed with intense severity. The capitalist could put his surplus paper money into the government lands and await results; but the men who needed their money from day to day suf-

---

* See Von Sybel, "History of the French Revolution," vol. i, pp. 281, 283.

† For proofs that issues of irredeemable paper at first stimulated manufactures and commerce in Austria and afterward ruined them, see Storch's "Economie politique," vol. iv, p. 223, note; and for the same effect produced by the same causes in Russia, see ibid., end of vol. iv. For the same effects in America, see Sumner's "History of American Currency." For general statement of effect of inconvertible issues on foreign exchanges see McLeod on "Banking," p. 186.

fered the worst of the misery. Still another difficulty appeared. There had come a complete uncertainty as to the future. Long before the close of 1791 no one knew whether a piece of paper money representing a hundred *livres* would, a month later, have a purchasing power of ninety or eighty or sixty *livres*. The result was that capitalists feared to embark their means in business. Enterprise received a mortal blow. Demand for labor was still further diminished; and here came a new cause of calamity: for this uncertainty withered all far-reaching undertakings. The business of France dwindled into a mere living from hand to mouth. This state of things, too, while it bore heavily upon the moneyed classes, was still more ruinous to those in moderate and, most of all, to those in straitened circumstances. With the masses of the people, the purchase of every article of supply became a speculation—a speculation in which the professional speculator had an immense advantage over the ordinary buyer. Says the most brilliant of apologists for French revolutionary statesmanship, "Commerce was dead; betting took its place." *

Nor was there any compensating advantage to the mercantile classes. The merchant was forced to add to his ordinary profit a sum sufficient to cover probable or possible fluctuations in value, and while prices of products thus went higher, the wages of labor, owing to the number of workmen who were thrown out of employment, went lower.

But these evils, though great, were small compared to those far more deep-seated signs of disease which now showed themselves throughout the country. One of these was the *obliteration of thrift* from the minds of the French people. The French are naturally thrifty; but, with such masses of money and with such uncertainty as to its future value, the ordinary motives for saving and care diminished, and a loose luxury spread throughout the country. A still worse outgrowth was the increase of speculation and gambling. With the plethora of paper currency in 1791 ap-

---

* See Louis Blanc, "Histoire de la Révolution," tome xii, p. 113.

peared the first evidences of that cancerous disease which always follows large issues of irredeemable currency,—a disease more permanently injurious to a nation than war, pestilence or famine. For at the great metropolitan centers grew a luxurious, speculative, stock-gambling body, which, like a malignant tumor, absorbed into itself the strength of the nation and sent out its cancerous fibres to the remotest hamlets. At these city centers abundant wealth seemed to be piled up: in the country at large there grew a dislike of steady labor and a contempt for moderate gains and simple living. In a pamphlet published in May, 1791, we see how, in regard to this also, public opinion was blinded. The author calls attention to the increase of gambling in values of all sorts in these words: "What shall I say of the stock-jobbing, as frightful as it is scandalous, which goes on in Paris under the very eyes of our legislators,—a most terrible evil, yet, under the present circumstances,—necessary?" The author also speaks of these stock-gamblers as using the most insidious means to influence public opinion in favor of their measures; and then proposes, seriously, a change in various matters of detail, thinking that this would prove a sufficient remedy for an evil which had its roots far down in the whole system of irredeemable currency. As well might a physician prescribe a pimple wash for a diseased liver.*

Now began to be seen more plainly some of the many ways in which an inflation policy robs the working class. As these knots of plotting schemers at the city centers were becoming bloated with sudden wealth, the producing classes of the country, though having in their possession more and more currency, grew lean. In the schemes and speculations put forth by stock-jobbers and stimulated by the printing of more currency, multitudes of small fortunes were absorbed and lost while a few swollen fortunes were rapidly aggregated in the larger cities. This crippled a large class

---

* See "Extrait du registre des délibérations de la section de la bibliothèque," May 3, 1791, pp. 4, 5.

in the country districts, which had employed a great number of workmen.

In the leading French cities now arose a luxury and license which was a greater evil even than the plundering which ministered to it. In the country the gambling spirit spread more and more. Says the same thoughtful historian whom I have already quoted: "What a prospect for a country when its rural population was changed into a great band of gamblers!" *

Nor was this reckless and corrupt spirit confined to business men; it began to break out in official circles, and public men who, a few years before, had been thought above all possibility of taint, became luxurious, reckless, cynical and finally corrupt. Mirabeau himself, who, not many months previous, had risked imprisonment and even death to establish constitutional government, was now—at this very time—secretly receiving heavy bribes. When, at the downfall of the monarchy a few years later, the famous iron chest of the Tuileries was opened, there were found evidences that, in this carnival of inflation and corruption, he had been a regularly paid servant of the Royal court.† The artful plundering of the people at large was bad enough, but worse still was this growing corruption in official and legislative circles. Out of the speculating and gambling of the inflation period grew luxury, and, out of this, corruption. It grew as naturally as a fungus on a muck heap. It was first felt in business operations, but soon began to be seen in the legislative body and in journalism. Mirabeau was, by no means, the only example. Such members of the legislative body as Jullien of Toulouse, Delaunay of Angers, Fabre d'Eglantine

---

* Von Sybel, vol. i, p. 273.

† For general account, see Thiers' "Révolution," chap. xiv; also Lacretelle, vol. viii, p. 109; also "Memoirs of Mallet du Pan." For a good account of the intrigues between the court and Mirabeau and of the prices paid him, see Reeve, "Democracy and Monarchy in France," vol. i, pp. 213-220. For a very striking caricature published after the iron chest in the Tuileries was opened and the evidences of bribery of Mirabeau fully revealed, see Challamel, "Musée," etc. Vol. i, p. 341, is represented as a skeleton sitting on a pile of letters, holding the French crown in one hand and a purse of gold in the other.

and their disciples, were among the most noxious of those conspiring by legislative action to raise and depress securities for stock-jobbing purposes. Bribery of legislators followed as a matter of course, Delaunay, Jullien and Chabot accepted a bribe of five hundred thousand *livres* for aiding legislation calculated to promote the purposes of certain stock-jobbers. It is some comfort to know that nearly all concerned were guillotined for it.*

It is true that the number of these corrupt legislators was small, far less than alarmists led the nation to suppose, but there were enough to cause wide-spread distrust, cynicism and want of faith in any patriotism or any virtue.

---

* Thiers, chap. ix.

II.

EVEN worse than this was the breaking down of the morals of the country at large, resulting from the sudden building up of ostentatious wealth in a few large cities, and from the gambling, speculative spirit spreading from these to the small towns and rural districts. From this was developed an even more disgraceful result,—the decay of a true sense of national good faith. The patriotism which the fear of the absolute monarchy, the machinations of the court party, the menaces of the army and the threats of all monarchical Europe had been unable to shake was gradually disintegrated by this same speculative, stock-jobbing habit fostered by the superabundant currency. At the outset, in the discussions preliminary to the first issue of paper money, Mirabeau and others who had favored it had insisted that patriotism as well as an enlightened self-interest, would lead the people to keep up the value of paper money. The very opposite of this was now revealed, for there appeared, as another outgrowth of this disease, what has always been seen under similar circumstances. It is a result of previous, and a cause of future evils. This outgrowth was a vast debtor class in the nation, directly interested in the depreciation of the currency in which they were to pay their debts. The nucleus of this class was formed by those who had purchased the church lands from the government. Only small payments down had been required and the remainder was to be paid in deferred installments: an indebtedness of a multitude of people had thus been created to the amount of hundreds of millions. This body of debtors soon saw, of course, that their interest was to depreciate the currency in which their debts were to be paid; and these were speedily joined by a far more influential class;—by that class whose speculative tendencies had been stimulated by the abundance of paper money, and who had gone largely into debt, looking for a rise in nominal values. Soon demagogues of the viler sort in the political clubs began to pander to it; a little later important persons in this debtor class were to be found intriguing in the Assembly—first in its seats and later in more conspicuous places of public trust. Before long, the debtor class became a powerful body extending through all ranks of society. From the stock-gambler who sat in the Assembly to the small land speculator in the rural districts; from the sleek inventor of *canards* on the Paris Exchange to the lying stock-jobber in the market town, all pressed vigorously for new issues of paper; all were apparently able to demonstrate to the people that in new issues of paper lay the only chance for national prosperity.

This great debtor class, relying on the multitude who could be approached by superficial arguments, soon gained control. Strange as it might seem to those who have not watched the same causes at work at a previous period in France and at various times in other countries, while every issue of paper money really made matters worse, a superstition gained ground among the people at large that, if only *enough* paper money were issued and were more cunningly handled the poor would be made rich. Henceforth, all opposition was futile. In December, 1791, a report was made in the Legislative Assembly in favor of yet another great issue of three hundred millions more of paper money. In regard to this report Cambon said that more money was needed but asked, "Will you, in a moment when stock-jobbing is carried on with such fury, give it new power by adding so much more to the circulation?" But such high considerations were now little regarded. Dorisy declared, "There is not enough money yet in circulation; if there were more the sales of national lands would be more rapid." And the official report of his speech states that these words were applauded.

Dorisy then went on to insist that the government lands were worth at least thirty-five hundred million *livres* and said: "Why should members ascend the tribunal and disquiet France? Fear nothing; your currency reposes upon a sound mortgage." Then followed a glorification of the patriotism of the French people, which, he asserted, would carry the nation through all its difficulties.

Becquet, speaking next, declared that "The circulation is becoming more rare every day."

On December 17, 1791, a new issue was ordered, making in all twenty-one hundred millions authorized. Coupled with this was the declaration that the total amount in actual circulation should never reach more than sixteen hundred millions. Before this issue the value of the 100 *livres* note had fallen at Paris to about 80 *livres;* * immediately afterward it fell to about 68 *livres.* What limitations of the currency were worth may be judged from the fact that not only had the declaration made hardly a year before, limiting the amount in circulation to twelve hundred millions, been violated, but the declaration, made hardly a month previous, in which the Assembly had as solemnly limited the amount of circulation to fourteen hundred millions, had also been repudiated.

The evils which we have already seen arising from the earlier issues were now aggravated; but the most curious thing evolved out of all this chaos was a *new system of political economy*. In speeches, newspapers and pamphlets about this time, we begin to find it declared that, after all, a depreciated currency is a blessing; that gold and silver form an unsatisfactory standard for measuring values: that it is a good thing to have a currency that will not go out of the kingdom and which separates France from other nations: that thus shall manufacturers be encouraged; that commerce with other nations may be a curse, and hindrance thereto may be a blessing; that the laws of political economy however applicable in other times, are not applicable to this particular period, and, however operative in other nations, are not now so in France; that the ordinary rules

---

* For this and other evidences of steady decline in the purchasing power of the *assignats,* see Caron, "Tableaux de Dépréciation du papier-monnaie," Paris, 1909, p. 386.

of political economy are perhaps suited to the minions of despotism but not to the free and enlightened inhabitants of France at the close of the eighteenth century; that the whole state of present things, so far from being an evil is a blessing. All these ideas, and others quite as striking, were brought to the surface in the debates on the various new issues.*

Within four months came another report to the Assembly as ingenious as those preceding. It declared: "Your committee are thoroughly persuaded that the amount of the circulating medium before the Revolution was greater than that of the *assignats* today: but at that time the money circulated slowly and now it passes rapidly so that one thousand million *assignats* do the work of two thousand millions of specie." The report foretells further increase in prices, but by some curious jugglery reaches a conclusion favorable to further inflation. Despite these encouragements the *assignats* nominally worth 100 *livres* had fallen, at the beginning of February, 1792, to about 60 *livres,* and during that month fell to 53 *livres.*†

In March, Clavière became minister of finance. He was especially proud of his share in the invention and advocacy of the *assignats,* and now pressed their creation more vigorously than ever, and on April 30th, of the same year, came the fifth great issue of paper money, amounting to three hundred millions: at about the same time Cambon sneered ominously at public creditors as "rich people, old financiers and bankers." Soon payment was suspended on dues to public creditors for all amounts exceeding ten thousand *francs.*

This was hailed by many as a measure in the interests of the poorer classes of people, but the result was that it in-

---

* See especially ''Discours de Fabre d'Eglantine,'' in ''Moniteur'' for August 11, 1793; also debate in ''Moniteur'' of September 15, 1793; also Prudhomme's ''Révolutions de Paris.'' For arguments of much the same tenor, see vast numbers of pamphlets, newspaper articles and speeches during the ''Greenback Craze,''—and the craze for unlimited coinage of silver,—in the United States.

† See Caron, ''Tableaux de Dépréciation,'' as above, p. 386.

jured them most of all. Henceforward, until the end of this
history, capital was quietly taken from labor and locked up
in all the ways that financial ingenuity could devise. All
that saved thousands of laborers in France from starvation
was that they were drafted off into the army and sent to be
killed on foreign battlefields.

On the last day of July, 1792, came another brilliant report from Fouquet, showing that the total amount of currency already issued was about twenty-four hundred millions, but claiming that the national lands were worth a
little more than this sum. A decree was now passed issuing
three hundred millions more. By this the prices of everything were again enhanced save one thing, and that one
thing was *labor*. Strange as it may at first appear, while
the depreciation of the currency had raised all products
enormously in price, the stoppage of so many manufactories
and the withdrawal of capital caused wages in the summer
of 1792, after all the inflation, to be as small as they had
been four years before—viz., fifteen *sous* per day. No more
striking example can be seen of the truth uttered by Daniel
Webster, that "of all the contrivances for cheating the laboring classes of mankind, none has been more effective than
that which deludes them with paper-money." *

Issue after issue followed at intervals of a few months,
until, on December 14, 1792, we have an official statement to
the effect that thirty-five hundred millions had been put
forth, of which six hundred millions had been burned, leaving in circulation twenty-eight hundred millions.

When it is remembered that there was little business to
do and that the purchasing power of the *livre* or *franc*,
when judged by the staple products of the country, was
equal to about half the present purchasing power of our own
dollar, it will be seen into what evils France had drifted. As
the mania for paper money ran its course, even the *sous*,
obtained by melting down the church bells, were more and
more driven out of circulation and more and more parch-

---

* Von Sybel, vol. i, pp. 509, 510, 515; also Villeneuve Bargemont,
"Histoire de l'Economie Politique," vol. ii, p. 213.

ment notes from twenty *four* to five were issued, and at
last pieces of one *sou*, of half a *sou* and even of one-quarter
of a *sou* were put in circulation.*

But now another source of wealth was opened to the nation. There came a confiscation of the large estates of landed
proprietors who had fled the country. An estimate in 1793
made the value of these estates three billions of *francs*. As
a consequence, the issues of paper money were continued in
increased amounts, on the old theory that they were guaranteed by the solemn pledge of these lands belonging to
the state. Under the Legislative Assembly through the year
1792 new issues were made virtually every month, so that
at the end of January, 1793, it was more and more realized
that the paper money actually in circulation amounted close
upon three thousand millions of *francs*. All this had been
issued publicly, in open sessions of the National and Legislative Assemblies; but now under the National Convention,
the two Committees of Public Safety and of Finance began
to decree new issues privately, in secret session.

As a result, the issues became larger still, and four hundred workmen were added to those previously engaged in
furnishing this paper money, and these were so pressed with
work from six o'clock in the morning until eight in the eve-
ning that they struck for higher wages and were successful.†

The consequences of these overissues now began to be
more painfully evident to the people at large. Articles of
common consumption became enormously dear and prices
were constantly rising. Orators in the Legislative Assembly,

---

* As to the purchasing power of money at that time, see Arthur
Young, ''Travels in France during the Years 1787, 1788 and 1789.''
For notices of the small currency with examples of satirical verses
written regarding it, see Challamel, ''Les Français sous la Révolution,'' pp. 307, 308. See also Mercier, ''Le Nouveau Paris,'' edition
of 1800, chapter ccv., entitled ''Parchemin Monnaie.'' A series of
these petty notes will be found in the White collection of the Cornell
University Library. They are very dirty and much worn, but being
printed on parchment, remain perfectly legible. For issue of quarter-
''*sou*'' pieces see Levasseur, p. 180.

† See Levasseur, vol. i, p. 176.

clubs, local meetings and elsewhere now endeavored to en-
lighten people by assigning every reason for this depreciation save the true one. They declaimed against the
corruption of the ministry, the want of patriotism among
the Moderates, the intrigues of the emigrant nobles, the
hard-heartedness of the rich, the monopolizing spirit of the
merchants, the perversity of the shopkeepers,—each and all
of these as causes of the difficulty.*

This decline in the government paper was at first somewhat masked by fluctuations. For at various times the value
of the currency *rose*. The victory of Jemappes and the general success of the French army against the invaders, with
the additional security offered by new confiscations of land,
caused, in November, 1792, an appreciation in the value of
the currency; the *franc* had stood at 57 and it rose to about
69; but the downward tendency was soon resumed and in
September, 1793, the *assignats* had sunk below 30. Then
sundry new victories and coruscations of oratory gave momentary confidence so that in December, 1793, they rose
above 50. But despite these fluctuations the downward
tendency soon became more rapid than ever.†

The washerwomen of Paris, finding soap so dear that they
could hardly purchase it, insisted that all the merchants who
were endeavoring to save something of their little property
by refusing to sell their goods for the wretched currency
with which France was flooded, should be punished with
death; the women of the markets and the hangers-on of the
Jacobin Club called loudly for a law "to equalize the value
of paper money and silver coin." It was also demanded that
a tax be laid especially on the rich, to the amount of four
hundred million *francs*, to buy bread. Marat declared loudly
that the people, by hanging shopkeepers and plundering
stores, could easily remove the trouble. The result was that
on the 28th of February, 1793, at eight o'clock in the eve-
ning, a mob of men and women in disguise began plundering

* For Chaumette's brilliant display of fictitious reasons for the decline see Thiers, Shoberl's translation, published by Bentley, vol.
iii, p. 248.

† For these fluctuations, see Caron, as above, p. 387.

the stores and shops of Paris. At first they demanded only bread; soon they insisted on coffee and rice and sugar; at last they seized everything on which they could lay their hands—cloth, clothing, groceries and luxuries of every kind. Two hundred such places were plundered. This was endured for six hours and finally order was restored only by a grant of seven million *francs* to buy off the mob. The new political economy was beginning to bear its fruits luxuriantly. A gaudy growth of it appeared at the City Hall of Paris when, in response to the complaints of the plundered merchants, Roux declared, in the midst of great applause, that "shopkeepers were only giving back to the people what they had hitherto robbed them of."

The mob having thus been bought off by concessions and appeased by oratory, the government gained time to think, and now came a series of amazing expedients,—and yet all perfectly logical.

Three of these have gained in French history an evil preeminence, and first of the three was the Forced Loan.

In view of the fact that the well-to-do citizens were thought to be lukewarm in their support of the politicans controlling the country, various demagogues in the National Convention, which had now succeeded the National, Constituent and Legislative Assemblies, found ample matter for denunciations long and loud. The result outside the Convention was increased activity of the guillotine; the results inside were new measures against all who had money, and on June 22, 1793, the Convention determined that there should be a Forced Loan, secured on the confiscated lands of the emigrants and levied upon all married men with incomes of ten thousand *francs,* and upon all unmarried men with incomes of six thousand *francs.* It was calculated that these would bring into the treasury a thousand millions of *francs.* But a difficulty was found. So many of the rich had fled or had concealed their wealth that only a fifth of the sum required could be raised, and therefore a law was soon passed which levied forced loans upon incomes as low as one thousand *francs,*—or, say, two hundred dollars of American money. This tax was made progressive. On the smaller proprietors it was fixed at one-tenth and on the larger, that is, on all incomes above nine thousand *francs,* it was made one-half of the entire income. Little if any provision was made for the repayment of this loan but the certificates might be used for purchasing the confiscated real estate of the church and of the nobility.*

But if this first expedient shows how naturally a "fiat" money system runs into despotism, the next is no less instructive in showing how easily it becomes repudiation and dishonor.

As we have seen, the first issue of the *assignats,*—made by the National Assembly,—bore a portrait of the king; but on the various issues after the establishment of a republic this emblem had been discarded. This change led to a difference in value between the earlier and the later paper money. The wild follies of fanatics and demagogues had led to an increasing belief that the existing state of things could not last; that the Bourbons must ere long return; that in such case, while a new monarch would repudiate all the vast mass of the later paper issued by the Republic, he would recognize that first issue bearing the face and therefore the guarantee of the king. So it was that this first issue came to bear a higher value than those of later date. To meet this condition of things it was now proposed to repudiate all that earlier issue. In vain did sundry more thoughtful members of the Convention plead that this paper money, amounting to five hundred and fifty-eight millions of *francs,* bore the solemn guarantee of the nation, as well as of the king; the current was irresistible. All that Cambon, the great leader of finance at that time, could secure was a clause claiming to protect the poor, to the effect that this demonetization should not extend to notes below a hundred *francs* in value; and it was also agreed that any of the notes, large

* One of the Forced Loan certificates will be found in the White Collection in the Library of Cornell University.

or small, might be received in payment of taxes and for
the confiscated property of the clergy and nobility. To all
the arguments advanced against this breach of the national
faith Danton, then at the height of his power, simply declared that only aristocrats could favor notes bearing the
royal portrait, and gave forth his famous utterance: "Imi-
tate Nature, which watches over the preservation of the
race but has no regard for individuals." The decree was
passed on the 31st of July, 1793, yet its futility was apparent in less than two months, when the Convention decreed
that there should be issued two thousand millions of *francs*
more in *assignats* between the values of ten *sous* and four
hundred *francs,* and when, before the end of the year, five
hundred millions more were authorized.*

The third outgrowth of the vast issue of fiat money was
the *Maximum.* As far back as November, 1792, the Terror-
ist associate of Robespierre, St. Just, in view of the steady
rise in prices of the necessaries of life, had proposed a
scheme by which these prices should be established by law,
at a rate proportionate to the wages of the working classes.
This plan lingered in men's minds, taking shape in various
resolutions and decrees until the whole culminated on September 29, 1793, in the Law of the *Maximum.*

While all this legislation was high-handed, it was not care-
less. Even statesmen of the greatest strength, having once
been drawn into this flood, were borne on into excesses
which, a little earlier, would have appalled them. Committees of experts were appointed to study the whole subject
of prices, and at last there were adopted the great "four
rules" which seemed to statesmen of that time a masterly
solution of the whole difficulty.†

---

* For details of these transactions, see Levasseur, as above, vol. i,
chap. 6, pp. 181, et seq. Original specimens of these notes, bearing
the portrait of Louis XVI will be found in the Cornell University Library (White Collection) and for the whole series perfectly photo-
graphed in the same collection, Dewarmin, ''Cent ans de numismatique
française,'' vol. i, pp. 143-165.

† For statements showing the distress and disorder that forced the
Convention to establish the *"Maximum"* see Levasseur, vol. i, pp.
188-193.

First, the price of each article of necessity was to be fixed at one and one-third its price in 1790. *Secondly,* all transportation was to be added at a fixed rate per league. *Thirdly,* five per cent was to be added for the profit of the wholesaler. *Fourthly,* ten per cent was to be added for the profit of the retailer. Nothing could look more reasonable. Great was the jubilation. The report was presented and supported by Barrère,—"the tiger monkey,"—then in all the glory of his great orations: now best known from his portrait by Macaulay. Nothing could withstand Barrère's eloquence. He insisted that France had been suffering from a *"Monarchical* commerce which only sought wealth," while what she needed and what she was now to receive was a *"Republican* commerce—a commerce of moderate profits and virtuous." He exulted in the fact that "France alone enjoys such a commerce,—that it exists in no other nation." He poured contempt over political economy as "that science which quacks have corrupted, which pedants have obscured and which academicians have depreciated." France, he said, has something better, and he declared in conclusion, "The needs of the people will no longer be spied upon in order that the commercial classes may arbitrarily take advantage." *

The first result of the *Maximum* was that every means was taken to evade the fixed price imposed, and the farmers brought in as little produce as they possibly could. This increased the scarcity, and the people of the large cities were put on an allowance. Tickets were issued authorizing the bearer to obtain at the official prices a certain amount of bread or sugar or soap or wood or coal to cover immediate necessities.†

But it was found that the *Maximum,* with its divinely revealed four rules, could not be made to work well—even by the shrewdest devices. In the greater part of France it could not be enforced. As to merchandise of foreign origin

---

* See Levasseur, as above, vol. i, pp. 195-225.
† See specimens of these tickets in the White Collection in the Cornell Library.

or merchandise into which any foreign product entered, the war had raised it far above the price allowed under the first rule, namely, the price of 1790, with an addition of one-third. Shopkeepers therefore could not sell such goods without ruin. The result was that very many went out of business and the remainder forced buyers to pay enormous charges under the very natural excuse that the seller risked his life in trading at all. That this excuse was valid is easily seen by the daily lists of those condemned to the guillotine, in which not infrequently figure the names of men charged with violating the *Maximum* laws. Manufactures were very generally crippled and frequently destroyed, and agriculture was fearfully depressed. To detect goods concealed by farmers and shopkeepers, a spy system was established with a reward to the informer of one-third of the value of the goods discovered. To spread terror, the Criminal Tribunal at Strassburg was ordered to destroy the dwelling of any one found guilty of selling goods above the price set by law. The farmer often found that he could not raise his products at anything like the price required by the new law, and when he tried to hold back his crops or cattle, alleging that he could not afford to sell them at the prices fixed by law, they were frequently taken from him by force and he was fortunate if paid even in the depreciated fiat money,—fortunate, indeed, if he finally escaped with his life.*

Involved in all these perplexities, the Convention tried to cut the Gordian knot. It decreed that any person selling gold or silver coin, or making any difference in any transaction between paper and specie, should be imprisoned in irons for six years:—that any one who refused to accept a payment in *assignats,* or accepted *assignats* at a discount, should pay a fine of three thousand *francs;* and that any one committing this crime a second time should pay a fine of six thousand *francs* and suffer imprisonment twenty years in irons. Later, on the 8th of September, 1793, the

---

* For these condemnations to the guillotine see the officially published trials and also the lists of the condemned, in the White Collection, also the lists given daily in the "Moniteur." For the spy system, see Levasseur, vol. i, p. 194.

penalty for such offences was made death, with confiscation of the criminal's property, and a reward was offered to any person informing the authorities regarding any such criminal transaction. To reach the climax of ferocity, the Convention decreed, in May, 1794, that the death penalty should be inflicted on any person convicted of "having asked, before a bargain was concluded, in what money payment was to be made." Nor was this all. The great finance minister, Cambon, soon saw that the worst enemies of his policy were gold and silver. Therefore it was that, under his lead, the Convention closed the Exchange and finally, on November 13, 1793, under terrifying penalties, suppressed all commerce in the precious metals. About a year later came the abolition of the *Maximum* itself.*

It is easily seen that these *Maximum* laws were perfectly logical. Whenever any nation intrusts to its legislators the issue of a currency not based on the idea of redemption in standard coin recognized in the commerce of civilized nations, it intrusts to them the power to raise or depress the value of every article in the possession of every citizen. Louis XIV had claimed that all property in France was his own, and that what private persons held was as much his as if it were in his coffers. But even this assumption is exceeded by the confiscating power exercised in a country, where, instead of leaving values to be measured by a standard common to the whole world, they are left to be depressed or raised at the whim, caprice or interest of a body of legislators. When this power is given, the power of fixing prices is inevitably included in it.†

---

* See Levasseur, as above, vol. i, p. 186. For an argument to show that the Convention was led into this Draconian legislation, not by necessity, but by its despotic tendencies, see Von Sybel's "History of the French Revolution," vol. iii, pp. 11, 12. For general statements of theories underlying the *"Maximum,"* see Thiers; for a very interesting picture, by an eye-witness, of the absurdities and miseries it caused, see Mercier, "Nouveau Paris," edition of 1800, chapter XLIV.

† For a summary of the report of the Committee, with list of articles embraced under it, and for various interesting details, see Villeneuve Bargemont, "Histoire de l'Economie Politique," vol. ii, pp. 213-239; also Levasseur, as above. For curious examples of severe

It may be said that these measures were made necessary by the war then going on. Nothing could be more baseless than such an objection. In this war the French soon became generally successful. It was quickly pushed mainly upon foreign soil. Numerous contributions were levied upon the subjugated countries to support the French armies. The war was one of those in which the loss, falling apparently on future generations, first stimulates, in a sad way, trade and production. The main cause of these evils was tampering with the circulating medium of an entire nation; keeping all values in fluctuation; discouraging enterprise; paralyzing energy; undermining sobriety; obliterating thrift; promoting extravagance and exciting riot by the issue of an irredeemable currency. The true business way of meeting the enormous demands on France during the first years of the Revolution had been stated by a true statesman and sound financier, Du Pont de Nemours, at the very beginning. He had shown that using the same paper as a circulating medium and as a means for selling the national real estate was like using the same implement for an oyster knife and a razor.*

It has been argued that the *assignats* sank in value because they were not well secured,—that securing them on government real estate was as futile as if the United States had, in the financial troubles of its early days, secured notes on its real estate. This objection is utterly fallacious. The government lands of our country were remote from the centers of capital and difficult to examine; the French national real estate was near these centers—even *in* them—and easy to examine. Our national real estate was unimproved and unproductive; theirs was improved and productive,—its

---

penalties for very slight infringements on the law on the subject, see Louis Blanc, ''Histoire de la Révolution française,'' tome x, p. 144. For Louis XIVth's claim see ''Memoirs of Louis XIV for the Instruction of the Dauphin.''

For a simple exposition of the way in which the exercise of this power became simply confiscation of all private property in France, see Mallet Du Pan's ''Memoirs,'' London, 1852, vol. ii, p. 14.

* See Du Pont's arguments, as given by Levasseur.

average productiveness in market in ordinary times being from four to five per cent.*

It has also been objected that the attempt to secure the *assignats* on government real estate failed because of the general want of confidence in the title derived by the purchasers from the new government. Every thorough student of that period must know that this is a misleading statement. Everything shows that the vast majority of the French people had a fanatical confidence in the stability of the new government during the greater part of the Revolution. There were disbelievers in the security of the *assignats* just as there were disbelievers in the paper money of the United States throughout our Civil War; but they were usually a small minority. Even granting that there was a doubt as to investment in French lands, the French people certainly had as much confidence in the secure possession of government lands as any people can ever have in large issues of government bonds: indeed, it is certain that they had far more confidence in their lands as a security than modern nations can usually have in large issues of bonds obtained by payments of irredeemable paper. One simple fact, as stated by John Stuart Mill, which made *assignats* difficult to convert into real estate was that the vast majority of people could not afford to make investments outside their business; and this fact is no less fatal to any attempt to contract large issues of irredeemable paper—save, perhaps, a bold, statesmanlike attempt, which seizes the best time and presses every advantage, eschewing all juggling devices and sacrificing everything to maintain a sound currency based on standards common to the entire financial world.

And now was seen, taking possession of the nation, that idea which developed so easily out of the fiat money system;—the idea that the ordinary needs of government may be legitimately met wholly by the means of paper currency;

* Louis Blanc calls attention to this very fact in showing the superiority of the French *assignats* to the old American Continental currency. See his "Histoire de la Révolution française," tome xii, p. 98.

—that taxes may be dispensed with. As a result, it was found that the *assignat* printing press was the one resource left to the government, and the increase in the volume of paper money became every day more appalling.

It will doubtless surprise many to learn that, in spite of these evident results of too much currency, the old cry of a "scarcity of circulating medium" was not stilled; it appeared not long after each issue, no matter how large.

But every thoughtful student of financial history knows that this cry always comes after such issues—nay, that it *must* come,—because in obedience to a natural law, the former scarcity, or rather *insufficiency* of currency recurs just as soon as prices become adjusted to the new volume, and there comes some little revival of business with the usual increase of credit.*

In August, 1793, appeared a new report by Cambon. No one can read it without being struck by its mingled ability and folly. His final plan of dealing with the public debt has outlasted all revolutions since, but his disposition of the inflated currency came to a wretched failure. Against Du Pont, who showed conclusively that the wild increase of paper money was leading straight to ruin, Cambon carried the majority in the great assemblies and clubs by sheer audacity—the audacity of desperation. Zeal in supporting the *assignats* became his religion. The National Convention which succeeded the Legislative Assembly, issued in 1793 over three thousand millions of *assignats,* and, of these, over twelve hundred millions were poured into the circulation. And yet Cambon steadily insisted that the security for the *assignat* currency was perfect. The climax of his zeal was reached when he counted as assets in the national treasury the indemnities which, he declared, France was sure to receive after future victories over the allied nations with which she was then waging a desperate war. As patriotism it was sublime; as finance it was deadly.†

---

* See Sumner, as above, p. 220.
† See Levasseur, as above, vol. i, p. 178.

Everything was tried. Very elaborately he devised a funding scheme which, taken in connection with his system of issues, was in effect what in these days would be called an *"interconvertibility scheme."* By various degrees of persuasion or force,—the guillotine looming up in the background,—holders of *assignats* were urged to convert them into evidence of national debt, bearing interest at five per cent, with the understanding that if more paper were afterward needed more would be issued. All in vain. The official tables of depreciation show that the *assignats* continued to fall. A forced loan, calling in a billion of these, checked this fall, but only for a moment. The *"interconvertibility scheme"* between currency and bonds failed as dismally as the *"interconvertibility scheme"* between currency and land had failed.*

A more effective expedient was a law confiscating the property of all Frenchmen who left France after July 14, 1789, and who had not returned. This gave new land to be mortgaged for the security of paper money.

All this vast chapter in financial folly is sometimes referred to as if it resulted from the direct action of men utterly unskilled in finance. This is a grave error. That wild schemers and dreamers took a leading part in setting the fiat money system going is true; that speculation and interested financiers made it worse is also true: but the men who had charge of French finance during the Reign of Terror and who made these experiments, which seem to us so monstrous, in order to rescue themselves and their country from the flood which was sweeping everything to financial ruin were universally recognized as among the most skillful and honest financiers in Europe. Cambon, especially, ranked then and ranks now as among the most expert in any period. The disastrous results of all his courage and ability in the attempt to stand against the deluge of paper money show

* See Cambon's "Report," Aug. 15, 1793, pp. 49-60; also, "Decree of Aug. 24, 1793," sec. 31, chapters XCVI-CIII. Also, "Tableaux de la dépréciation de papier monnaie dans le department de la Seine."

how powerless are the most skillful masters of finance to stem the tide of fiat money calamity when once it is fairly under headway; and how useless are all enactments which they can devise against the underlying laws of nature.

Month after month, year after year new issues went on. Meanwhile everything possible was done to keep up the value of paper. The city authorities of Metz took a solemn oath that the *assignats* should bear the same price whether in paper or specie,—and whether in buying or selling, and various other official bodies throughout the nation followed this example. In obedience to those who believed with the market women of Paris, as stated in their famous petition, that "laws should be passed making paper money as good as gold," Couthon, in August, 1793, had proposed and carried a law punishing any person who should sell *assignats* at less than their nominal value with imprisonment for twenty years in chains, and later carried a law making investments in foreign countries by Frenchmen punishable with death.*

But to the surprise of the great majority of the French people, the value of the *assignats* was found, after the momentary spasm of fear had passed, not to have been permanently increased by these measures: on the contrary, this "fiat" paper persisted in obeying the natural laws of finance and, as new issues increased, their value decreased. Nor did the most lavish aid of nature avail. The paper money of the nation seemed to possess a magic power to transmute prosperity into adversity and plenty into famine. The year 1794 was exceptionally fruitful: and yet with the autumn came scarcity of provisions and with the winter came distress. The reason is perfectly simple. The sequences in that whole history are absolutely logical. First, the Assembly had inflated the currency and raised prices enormously. Next, it had been forced to establish an arbitrary maximum price for produce. But this price, large as it seemed, soon fell below the real value of produce; many of the farmers,

---

* For the example of Metz and other authorities, see Levasseur, as above, vol. i, p. 180.

therefore, raised less produce or refrained from bringing
what they had to market.* But, as is usual in such cases,
the trouble was ascribed to everything rather than the real
cause, and the most severe measures were established in all
parts of the country to force farmers to bring produce to
market, millers to grind and shopkeepers to sell it.† The
issues of paper money continued. Toward the end of 1794
seven thousand millions in *assignats* were in circulation.‡
By the end of May, 1795, the circulation was increased to
ten thousand millions, at the end of July, to fourteen thousand millions; and the value of one hundred *francs* in paper
fell steadily, first to four *francs* in gold, then to three, then
to two and one-half.§ But, curiously enough, while this depreciation was rapidly going on, as at various other periods
when depreciation was rapid, there came an apparent revival of business. The hopes of many were revived by the
fact that in spite of the decline of paper there was an exceedingly brisk trade in all kinds of permanent property.
Whatever articles of permanent value certain needy people
were willing to sell certain cunning people were willing to
buy and to pay good prices for in *assignats*. At this, hope
revived for a time in certain quarters. But ere long it was
discovered that this was one of the most distressing results
of a natural law which is sure to come into play under such
circumstances. It was simply a feverish activity caused by
the intense desire of a large number of the shrewder class
to convert their paper money into anything and everything
which they could hold and hoard until the collapse which
they foresaw should take place. This very activity in business simply indicated the disease. It was simply legal robbery
of the more enthusiastic and trusting by the more cold-

---

* See Von Sybel, vol. iii, p. 173.
† See Thiers; also, for curious details of measures taken to compel
farmers and merchants, see Senior, Lectures on ''Results of Paper
Money,'' pp. 86, 87.
‡ See Von Sybel, vol. iv, p. 231.
§ See Von Sybel, vol. iv, p. 330; also tables of depreciation in
''Moniteur''; also official reports in the White Collection; also
Caron's ''Tables,'' etc.

hearted and keen. It was the "unloading" of the *assignats* upon the mass of the people.*

Interesting is it to note in the midst of all this the steady action of another simple law in finance. Prisons, guillotines, enactments inflicting twenty years' imprisonment in chains upon persons twice convicted of buying or selling paper money at less than its nominal value, and death upon investors in foreign securities, were powerless. The National Convention, fighting a world in arms and with an armed revolt on its own soil, showed titanic power, but in its struggle to circumvent one simple law of nature its weakness was pitiable. The *louis d'or* stood in the market as a monitor, noting each day, with unerring fidelity, the decline in value of the *assignat;* a monitor not to be bribed, not to be scared. As well might the National Convention try to bribe or scare away the polarity of the mariner's compass. On August 1, 1795, this gold *louis* of 25 *francs* was worth in paper, 920 *francs;* on September 1st, 1,200 *francs;* on November 1st, 2,600 *francs;* on December 1st, 3,050 *francs.* In February, 1796, it was worth 7,200 *francs* or one *franc* in gold was worth 288 *francs* in paper. Prices of all commodities went up nearly in proportion.† The writings of this period give curious details. Thibaudeau, in his Memoirs, speaks of sugar as 500 *francs* a pound, soap, 230 *francs,* candles, 140 *francs.* Mercier, in his lifelike pictures of the French metropolis at that period, mentions 600 *francs* as carriage hire for a single drive, and 6,000 for an entire day. Examples from other sources are such as the following:—a measure of flour advanced from two *francs* in 1790, to 225 *francs* in 1795; a pair of shoes, from five *francs* to 200; a

---

* For a lifelike sketch of the way in which these exchanges of *assignats* for valuable property went on at periods of the rapid depreciation of paper, see Challamel, "Les français sous la Révolution," p. 309; also Say "Economie Politique."

† For a very complete table of the depreciation from day to day, see "Supplement to the Moniteur" of October 2, 1797; also Caron, as above. For the market prices of the *louis d'or* at the first of every month, as the collapse approached, see Montgaillard. See also "Official Lists" in the White Collection. For a table showing the steady rise of the *franc* in gold during a single week, from 251 to 280 *francs,* see Dewarmin, as above, vol. i, p. 136.

hat, from 14 *francs* to 500; butter, to 560 *francs* a pound; a
turkey, to 900 *francs*.* Everything was enormously inflated
in price *except the wages of labor*. As manufacturers had
closed, wages had fallen, until all that kept them up seemed
to be the fact that so many laborers were drafted off into
the army. From this state of things came grievous wrong
and gross fraud. Men who had foreseen these results and
had gone into debt were of course jubilant. He who in 1790
had borrowed 10,000 *francs* could pay his debts in 1796 for
about 35 *francs*. Laws were made to meet these abuses. As
far back as 1794 a plan was devised for publishing official
"tables of depreciation" to be used in making equitable set-
tlements of debts, but all such machinery proved futile. On
the 18th of May, 1796, a young man complained to the National Convention that his elder brother, who had been
acting as administrator of his deceased father's estate, had
paid the heirs in *assignats,* and that he had received
scarcely one three-hundredth part of the real value of his
share.† To meet cases like this, a law was passed establish-
ing a "scale of proportion." Taking as a standard the value
of the *assignat* when there were two billions in circulation,
this law declared that, in payment of debts, one-quarter
should be added to the amount originally borrowed for
every five hundred millions added to the circulation. In
obedience to this law a man who borrowed two thousand
francs when there were two billions in circulation would
have to pay his creditors twenty-five hundred *francs* when
half a billion more were added to the currency, and over
thirty-five thousand *francs* before the emissions of paper
reached their final amount. This brought new evils, worse,
if possible, than the old.‡

---

* See "Mèmoires de Thibaudeau," vol. ii, p. 26, also Mercier, "Le
Nouveau Paris," vol. ii, p. 90; for curious example of the scales of
depreciation see the White Collection. See also extended table of
comparative values in 1790 and 1795. See Levasseur, as above, vol. i,
pp. 223-4.

† For a striking similar case in our own country, see Sumner, "History of American Currency," p. 47.

‡ See Villeneuve Bargemont, "Histoire de l'économie politique,"
vol. ii, p. 229.

The question will naturally be asked, *On whom did this vast depreciation mainly fall at last?* When this currency had sunk to about one three-hundredth part of its nominal value and, after that, to nothing, in whose hands was the bulk of it? The answer is simple. I shall give it in the exact words of that thoughtful historian from whom I have already quoted: "Before the end of the year 1795 the paper money was almost exclusively in the hands of the working classes, employees and men of small means, whose property was not large enough to invest in stores of goods or national lands.* Financiers and men of large means were shrewd enough to put as much of their property as possible into objects of permanent value. The working classes had no such foresight or skill or means. On them finally came the great crushing weight of the loss. After the first collapse came up the cries of the starving. Roads and bridges were neglected; many manufactures were given up in utter helplessness." To continue, in the words of the historian already cited: "None felt any confidence in the future in any respect; few dared to make a business investment for any length of time and it was accounted a folly to curtail the pleasures of the moment,—to accumulate or save for so uncertain a future." †

This system in finance was accompanied by a system in politics no less startling, and each system tended to aggravate the other. The wild radicals, having sent to the guillotine first all the Royalists and next all the leading Republicans they could entrap, the various factions began sending each other to the same destination:—Hébertists, Dantonists, with various other factions and groups, and, finally, the Robespierrists, followed each other in rapid succession. After these declaimers and phrase-mongers had thus disappeared there came to power, in October, 1795, a new

---

* See Von Sybel, vol. iv, pp. 337, 338. See also for confirmation Challamel, "Histoire Musée," vol. ii, p. 179. For a thoughtful statement of the reasons why such paper was not invested in lands by men of moderate means, and workingmen, see Mill, "Political Economy," vol. ii, pp. 81, 82.

† See Von Sybel, vol. iv, p. 222.

government,—mainly a survival of the more scoundrelly,—
the Directory. It found the country utterly impoverished
and its only resource at first was to print more paper and
to issue even while wet from the press. These new issues
were made at last by the two great committees, with or
without warrant of law, and in greater sums than ever.
Complaints were made that the army of engravers and
printers at the mint could not meet the demand for *assignats*—that they could produce only from sixty to
seventy millions per day and that the government was
spending daily from eighty to ninety millions. Four thousand millions of *francs* were issued during one month, a
little later three thousand millions, a little later four thousand millions, until there had been put forth over thirty-
five thousand millions. The purchasing power of this paper
having now become almost nothing, it was decreed, on the
22nd of December, 1795, that the whole amount issued
should be limited to forty thousand millions, including all
that had previously been put forth and that when this had
been done the copper plates should be broken. Even in spite
of this, additional issues were made amounting to about ten
thousand millions. But on the 18th of February, 1796, at
nine o'clock in the morning, in the presence of a great
crowd, the machinery, plates and paper for printing *assignats* were brought to the Place Vendome and there,
on the spot where the Napoleon Column now stands, these
were solemnly broken and burned.

Shortly afterward a report by Camus was made to the
Assembly that the entire amount of paper money issued in
less than six years by the Revolutionary Government of
France had been over forty-five thousand millions of *francs;*
that over six thousand millions had been annulled and
burned and that at the final catastrophe there were in circulation close upon forty thousand millions. It will be
readily seen that it was fully time to put an end to the
system, for the gold *"louis"* of twenty-five *francs* in specie
had, in February, 1796, as we have seen, become worth 7,200
francs, and, at the latest quotation of all, no less than

15,000 *francs* in paper money,—that is, one *franc* in gold was nominally worth 600 *francs* in paper.

Such were the results of allowing dreamers, schemers, phrase-mongers, declaimers and strong men subservient to these to control a government.*

---

* See especially Levasseur, ''Histoire des classes ouvrières,'' etc. vol. i, pp. 219, 230 and elsewhere; also De Nervo, ''Finance française,'' p. 280; also Stourm, as already cited. The exact amount of *assignats* in circulation at the final suppression is given by De-warmin, (vol. i, p. 189), as 39,999,945,428 *livres* or *francs*.

III.

THE first new expedient of the Directory was to secure a forced loan of six hundred million francs from the wealthier classes; but this was found fruitless. Ominous it was when persons compelled to take this loan found for an *assignat* of one hundred *francs* only one *franc* was allowed. Next a National Bank was proposed; but capitalists were loath to embark in banking while the howls of the mob against all who had anything especially to do with money resounded in every city. At last the Directory bethought themselves of another expedient. This was by no means new. It had been fully tried on our continent twice before that time: and once, since—first, in our colonial period; next, during our Confederation; lastly, by the "Southern Confederacy" and here, as elsewhere, always in vain. But experience yielded to theory—plain business sense to financial metaphysics. It was determined to issue a new paper which should be "fully secured" and "as good as gold."

Pursuant to this decision it was decreed that a new paper money "fully secured and as good as gold" be issued under the name of "*mandats*." In order that these new notes should be "fully secured," choice public real estate was set apart to an amount fully equal to the nominal value of the issue, and any one offering any amount of the *mandats* could at once take possession of government lands; the price of the lands to be determined by two experts, one named by the government and one by the buyer, and without the formalities and delays previously established in regard to the purchase of lands with *assignats*.

Perhaps the most whimsical thing in the whole situation was the fact that the government, pressed as it was by de-

mands of all sorts, continued to issue the old *assignats* at
the same time that it was discrediting them by issuing the
new *mandats*. And yet in order to make the *mandats* "as
good as gold" it was planned by forced loans and other
means to reduce the quantity of *assignats* in circulation, so
that the value of each *assignat* should be raised to one-
thirtieth of the value of gold, then to make *mandats* legal
tender and to substitute them for *assignats* at the rate of
one for thirty. Never were great expectations more cruelly
disappointed. Even before the *mandats* could be issued from
the press they fell to thirty-five per cent of their nominal
value; from this they speedily fell to fifteen, and soon after
to five per cent, and finally, in August, 1796, six months
from their first issue, to three per cent. This plan failed—
just as it failed in New England in 1737; just as it failed
under our own Confederation in 1781; just as it failed under
the Southern Confederacy during our Civil War.*

To sustain this new currency the government resorted to
every method that ingenuity could devise. Pamphlets suited
to people of every capacity were published explaining its
advantages. Never was there more skillful puffing. A pamphlet signed "Marchant" and dedicated to "People of Good
Faith" was widely circulated, in which Marchant took pains
to show the great advantage of the *mandats* as compared
with *assignats;*—how land could be more easily acquired
with them; how their security was better than with
assignats; how they could not, by any possibility, sink
in values as the *assignats* had done. But even before the
pamphlet was dry from the press the depreciation of the
mandats had refuted his entire argument.†

---

* For details of the *mandat* system very thoroughly given, see
Thiers' "History of the French Revolution," Bentley's edition, vol.
iv, pp. 410-412. For the issue of *assignats* and *mandats* at the same
time, see Dewarmin, vol. i, p. 136; also Levasseur, vol. i, pp. 230-
257. For an account of "new tenor bills" in America and their failure
in 1737, see Sumner, pp. 27-31; for their failure in 1781, see Morse,
"Life of Alexander Hamilton," vol. i, pp. 86, 87. For similar failure
in Austria, see Sumner, p. 314.

† See Marchant, "Lettre aux gens de bonne foi."

The old plan of penal measures was again pressed. Monot led off by proposing penalties against those who shall speak publicly against the *mandats;* Talot thought the penalties ought to be made especially severe; and finally it was enacted that any persons "who by their discourse or writing shall decry the *mandats* shall be condemned to a fine of not less than one thousand *francs* or more than ten thousand; and in case of a repetition of the offence, to four years in irons." It was also decreed that those who refused to receive the *mandats* should be fined,—the first time, the exact sum which they refuse; the second time, ten times as much; and the third time, punished with two years in prison. But here, too, came in the action of those natural laws which are alike inexorable in all countries. This attempt proved futile in France just as it had proved futile less than twenty years before in America. No enactments could stop the downward tendency of this new paper "fully secured," "as good as gold"; the laws that finally govern finance are not made in conventions or congresses.*

From time to time various new financial juggles were tried, some of them ingenious, most of them drastic. It was decreed that all *assignats* above the value of one hundred *francs* should cease to circulate after the beginning of June, 1796. But this only served to destroy the last vestige of confidence in government notes of any kind. Another expedient was seen in the decree that paper money should be made to accord with a natural and immutable standard of value and that one *franc* in paper should thenceforth be worth ten pounds of wheat. This also failed. On July 16th another decree seemed to show that the authorities despaired of regulating the existing currency and it was decreed that all paper, whether *mandats* or *assignats,* should be taken at its real value, and that bargains might be made in whatever currency people chose. The real value of the *mandats* speedily sank to about two per cent of

---

* See Sumner, p. 44; also De Nervo, ''Finances françaises,'' p. 282.

their nominal value and the only effect of this legislation seemed to be that both *assignats* and *mandats* went still lower. Then from February 4 to February 14, 1797, came decrees and orders that the engraving apparatus for the *mandats* should be destroyed as that for the *assignats* had been, that neither *assignats* nor *mandats* should longer be a legal tender and that old debts to the state might be paid for a time with government paper at the rate of one per cent of their face value.* Then, less than three months later, it was decreed that the twenty-one billions of *assignats* still in circulation should be annulled. Finally, on September 30, 1797, as the culmination of these and various other experiments and expedients, came an order of the Directory that the national debts should be paid two-thirds in bonds which might be used in purchasing confiscated real estate, and the remaining "Consolidated Third," as it was called, was to be placed on the "Great Book" of the national debt to be paid thenceforth as the government should think best.

As to the bonds which the creditors of the nation were thus forced to take, they sank rapidly, as the *assignats* and *mandats* had done, even to three per cent of their value. As to the "Consolidated Third," that was largely paid, until the coming of Bonaparte, in paper money which sank gradually to about six per cent of its face value. Since May, 1797, both *assignats* and *mandats* had been virtually worth nothing.

So ended the reign of paper money in France. The twenty-five hundred millions of *mandats* went into the common heap of refuse with the previous forty-five thousand millions of *assignats:* the nation in general, rich and poor alike, was plunged into financial ruin from one end to the other.

On the prices charged for articles of ordinary use light is thrown by extracts from a table published in 1795, reduced to American coinage.

---

* See De Nervo, "Finances françaises," p. 282; also Levasseur, vol. i, p. 236 et seq.

	1790	1795
For a bushel of flour	40 cents	45 dollars
For a bushel of oats	18 cents	10 dollars
For a cartload of wood	4 dollars	500 dollars
For a bushel of coal	7 cents	2 dollars
For a pound of sugar	18 cents	12½ dollars
For a pound of soap	18 cents	8 dollars
For a pound of candles	18 cents	8 dollars
For one cabbage	8 cents	5½ dollars
For a pair of shoes	1 dollar	40 dollars
For twenty-five eggs	24 cents	5 dollars

But these prices about the middle of 1795 were moderate compared with those which were reached before the close of that year and during the year following. Perfectly authentic examples were such as the following:

A pound of bread	9 dollars
A bushel of potatoes	40 dollars
A pound of candles	40 dollars
A cartload of wood	250 dollars

So much for the poorer people. Typical of those esteemed wealthy may be mentioned a manufacturer of hardware who, having retired from business in 1790 with 321,000 *livres,* found his property in 1796 worth 14,000 *francs.**

For this general distress arising from the development and collapse of "fiat" money in France, there was, indeed, one exception. In Paris and a few of the other great cities, men like Tallien, of the heartless, debauched, luxurious, speculator, contractor and stock-gambler class, had risen above the ruins of the multitudes of smaller fortunes. Tallien, one of the worst demagogue "reformers," and a certain number of men like him, had been skillful enough to become millionaires, while their dupes, who had clamored for issues of paper money, had become paupers.

The luxury and extravagance of the currency gamblers

---

* See Table from ''Gazette de France'' and extracts from other sources in Levasseur, vol. i, pp. 223-4.

and their families form one of the most significant features in any picture of the social condition of that period.*

A few years before this the leading women in French society showed a nobility of character and a simplicity in dress worthy of Roman matrons. Of these were Madame Roland and Madame Desmoulins; but now all was changed. At the head of society stood Madame Tallien and others like her, wild in extravagance, daily seeking new refinements in luxury, and demanding of their husbands and lovers vast sums to array them and to feed their whims. If such sums could not be obtained honestly they must be had dishonestly. The more closely one examines that period, the more clearly he sees that the pictures given by Thibaudeau and Challamel and De Goncourt are not at all exaggerated.†

The contrast between these gay creatures of the Directory period and the people at large was striking. Indeed much as the vast majority of the wealthy classes suffered from impoverishment, the laboring classes, salaried employees of all sorts, and people of fixed income and of small means, especially in the cities, underwent yet greater distress. These were found, as a rule, to subsist mainly on daily government rations of bread at the rate of one pound per person. This was frequently unfit for food and was distributed to long lines of people, men, women and children, who were at times obliged to wait their turn even from dawn to dusk. The very rich could, by various means, especially by bribery, obtain better bread, but only at enormous cost. In May, 1796, the market price of good bread was, in paper, 80 *francs*

---

* Among the many striking accounts of the debasing effects of "inflation" upon France under the Directory perhaps the best is that of Lacretelle, vol. xiii, pp. 32-36. For similar effect, produced by the same cause in our own country in 1819, see statement from Niles' "Register," in Sumner, p. 80. For the jumble of families reduced to beggary with families lifted into sudden wealth and for the mass of folly and misery thus mingled, see Levasseur, vol. i, p. 237.

† For Madame Tallien and luxury of the stock-gambler classes, see Challamel, "Les français sous la Révolution," pp. 30, 33; also De Goncourt, "Les français sous le Directoire." Regarding the outburst of vice in Paris and the demoralization of the police, see Levasseur, as above.

(16 dollars) per pound and a little later provisions could not be bought for paper money at any price.*

And here it may be worth mentioning that there was another financial trouble especially vexatious. While, as we have seen, such enormous sums, rising from twenty to forty thousand millions of *francs* in paper, were put in circulation by the successive governments of the Revolution, enormous sums had been set afloat in counterfeits by criminals and by the enemies of France. These came not only from various parts of the French Republic but from nearly all the surrounding nations, the main source being London. Thence it was that Count Joseph de Puisaye sent off cargoes of false paper, excellently engraved and printed, through ports in Brittany and other disaffected parts of France. One seizure by General Hoche was declared by him to exceed in nominal value ten thousand millions of *francs*. With the exception of a few of these issues, detection was exceedingly difficult, even for experts; for the vast majority of the people it was impossible.

Nor was this all. At various times the insurgent royalists in La Vendee and elsewhere put *their* presses also in operation, issuing notes bearing the Bourbon arms,—the *fleur-de-lis,* the portrait of the Dauphin (as Louis XVII) with the magic legend *"De Par le Roi,"* and large bodies of the population in the insurgent districts were *forced* to take these. Even as late as 1799 these notes continued to appear.†

The financial agony was prolonged somewhat by attempts to secure funds by still another "forced loan," and other discredited measures, but when all was over with paper

---

* See Levasseur, vol. i, p. 237, et seq.

† For specimens of counterfeit *assignats,* see the White Collection in the Cornell University Library, but for the great series of various issues of them in fac-simile, also for detective warnings and attempted descriptions of many varieties of them, and for the history of their issue, see especially Dewarmin, vol. i, pp. 152-161. For photographic copies of Royalist *assignats,* etc., see also Dewarmin, ibid., pp. 192-197, etc. For a photograph of probably the last of the Royalist notes ever issued, bearing the words ''Pro Deo, pro Rege, pro Patria'' and ''Armée Catholique et Royale'' with the date 1799, and for the sum of 100 *livres,* see Dewarmin, vol. i, p. 204.

money, specie began to reappear—first in sufficient sums
to do the small amount of business which remained after
the collapse. Then as the business demand increased, the
amount of specie flowed in from the world at large to meet
it and the nation gradually recovered from that long paper-
money debauch.

Thibaudeau, a very thoughtful observer, tells us in his
Memoirs that great fears were felt as to a want of circulating medium between the time when paper should go out and
coin should come in; but that no such want was severely
felt—that coin came in gradually as it was wanted.*

Nothing could better exemplify the saying of one of the
most shrewd of modern statesmen that "There will always
be money." †

But though there soon came a degree of prosperity—as
compared with the distress during the paper-money orgy,—
convalescence was slow. The acute suffering from the wreck
and ruin brought by *assignats, mandats* and other paper
currency in process of repudiation lasted nearly ten years,
but the period of recovery lasted longer than the generation
which followed. It required fully forty years to bring capital, industry, commerce and credit up to their condition
when the Revolution began, and demanded a "man on horse-
back," who established monarchy on the ruins of the Republic and thew away millions of lives for the Empire, to
be added to the millions which had been sacrificed by the
Revolution.‡

Such, briefly sketched in its leading features, is the history of the most skillful, vigorous and persistent attempt
ever made to substitute for natural laws in finance the
ability of legislative bodies, and, for a standard of value
recognized throughout the world, a national standard devised by theorists and manipulated by schemers. Every
other attempt of the same kind in human history, under

---

* For similar expectation of a "shock," which did not occur, at
the resumption of specie payments in Massachusetts, see Sumner,
"History of American Currency," p. 34.

† See Thiers.

‡ See Levasseur, vol. i, p. 246.

whatever circumstances, has reached similar results in kind if not in degree; all of them show the existence of financial laws as real in their operation as those which hold the planets in their courses.*

I have now presented this history in its *chronological* order—the order of events: let me, in conclusion, sum it up, briefly, in its *logical* order,—the order of cause and effect.

And, first, in the *economic* department. From the early reluctant and careful issues of paper we saw, as an immediate result, improvement and activity in business. Then arose the clamor for more paper money. At first, new issues were made with great difficulty; but, the dyke once broken, the current of irredeemable currency poured through; and, the breach thus enlarging, this currency was soon swollen beyond control. It was urged on by speculators for a rise in values; by demagogues who persuaded the mob that a nation, by its simple fiat, could stamp real value to any amount upon valueless objects. As a natural consequence a great debtor class grew rapidly, and this class gave its influence to depreciate more and more the currency in which its debts were to be paid.†

The government now began, and continued by spasms to grind out still more paper; commerce was at first stimulated by the difference in exchange; but this cause soon ceased to operate, and commerce, having been stimulated unhealthfully, wasted away.

Manufactures at first received a great impulse; but, ere long, this overproduction and overstimulus proved as fatal to them as to commerce. From time to time there was a

---

* For examples of similar effects in Russia, Austria and Denmark, see Storch, "Economie Politique," vol. iv; for similar effects in the United States, see Gouge, "Paper Money and Banking in the United States," also Sumner, "History of American Currency." For working out of the same principles in England, depicted in a masterly way, see Macaulay, "History of England," chap. xxi; and for curious exhibition of the same causes producing same results in ancient Greece, see a curious quotation by Macaulay in same chapter.

† For parallel cases in the early history of our own country, see Sumner, p. 21, and elsewhere.

revival of hope caused by an apparent revival of business; but this revival of business was at last seen to be caused more and more by the desire of far-seeing and cunning men of affairs to exchange paper money for objects of permanent value. As to the people at large, the classes living on fixed incomes and small salaries felt the pressure first, as soon as the purchasing power of their fixed incomes was reduced. Soon the great class living on wages felt it even more sadly.

Prices of the necessities of life increased: merchants were obliged to increase them, not only to cover depreciation of their merchandise, but also to cover their risk of loss from fluctuation; and, while the prices of products thus rose, wages, which had at first gone up, under the general stimulus, lagged behind. Under the universal doubt and discouragement, commerce and manufactures were checked or destroyed. As a consequence the demand for labor was diminished; laboring men were thrown out of employment, and, under the operation of the simplest law of supply and demand, the price of labor—the daily wages of the laboring class—went down until, at a time when prices of food, clothing and various articles of consumption were enormous, wages were nearly as low as at the time preceding the first issue of irredeemable currency.

The mercantile classes at first thought themselves exempt from the general misfortune. They were delighted at the apparent advance in the value of the goods upon their shelves. But they soon found that, as they increased prices to cover the inflation of currency and the risk from fluctuation and uncertainty, purchases became less in amount and payments less sure; a feeling of insecurity spread throughout the country; enterprise was deadened and stagnation followed.

New issues of paper were then clamored for as more drams are demanded by a drunkard. New issues only increased the evil; capitalists were all the more reluctant to embark their money on such a sea of doubt. Workmen of all sorts were more and more thrown out of employment. Issue after issue of currency came; but no relief resulted save a momentary stimulus, which aggravated the disease. The most ingenious evasions of natural laws in finance which the most subtle theorists could contrive were tried—all in vain; the most brilliant substitutes for those laws were tried; "self-regulating" schemes, "interconverting" schemes —all equally vain.* All thoughtful men had lost confidence. All men were *waiting;* stagnation became worse and worse. At last came the collapse and then a return, by a fearful shock, to a state of things which presented something like certainty of remuneration to capital and labor. Then, and not till then, came the beginning of a new era of prosperity.

Just as dependent on the law of cause and effect was the *moral* development. Out of the inflation of prices grew a speculating class; and, in the complete uncertainty as to the future, all business became a game of chance, and all business men, gamblers. In city centers came a quick growth of stock-jobbers and speculators; and these set a debasing fashion in business which spread to the remotest parts of the country. Instead of satisfaction with legitimate profits, came a passion for inordinate gains. Then, too, as values became more and more uncertain, there was no longer any motive for care or economy, but every motive for immediate expenditure and present enjoyment. So came upon the nation the *obliteration of thrift.* In this mania for yielding to present enjoyment rather than providing for future comfort were the seeds of new growths of wretchedness: luxury, senseless and extravagant, set in: this, too, spread as a fashion. To feed it, there came cheatery in the nation at large and corruption among officials and persons holding trusts. While men set such fashions in private and official business, women set fashions of extravagance in dress and living that added to the incentives to corruption. Faith in moral considerations, or even in good impulses, yielded to general distrust. National honor was thought a fiction cher-

---

* For a review of some of these attempts, with eloquent statement of their evil results, see ''Mémoires de Durand de Maillane,'' pp. 166-169.

ished only by hypocrites. Patriotism was eaten out by cynicism.

Thus was the history of France logically developed in obedience to natural laws; such has, to a greater or less degree, always been the result of irredeemable paper, created according to the whim or interest of legislative assemblies rather than based upon standards of value permanent in their nature and agreed upon throughout the entire world. Such, we may fairly expect, will always be the result of them until the fiat of the Almighty shall evolve laws in the universe radically different from those which at present obtain.*

And, finally, as to the general development of the theory and practice which all this history records: my subject has been Fiat Money in France; How it came; What it brought; and How it ended.

It came by seeking a remedy for a comparatively small evil in an evil infinitely more dangerous. To cure a disease temporary in its character, a corrosive poison was administered, which ate out the vitals of French prosperity.

It progressed according to a law in social physics which we may call the *"law of accelerating issue and depreciation."* It was comparatively easy to refrain from the first issue; it was exceedingly difficult to refrain from the second; to refrain from the third and those following was practically impossible.

It brought, as we have seen, commerce and manufactures, the mercantile interest, the agricultural interest, to ruin. It brought on these the same destruction which would come to a Hollander opening the dykes of the sea to irrigate his garden in a dry summer.

It ended in the complete financial, moral and political prostration of France—a prostration from which only a Napoleon could raise it.

---

* For similar effect of inflated currency in enervating and undermining trade, husbandry, manufactures and morals in our own country, see Daniel Webster, cited in Sumner, pp. 45-50. For similar effects in other countries, see Senior, Storch, Macaulay and others already cited.

But this history would be incomplete without a brief sequel, showing how that great genius profited by all his experience. When Bonaparte took the consulship the condition of fiscal affairs was appalling. The government was bankrupt; an immense debt was unpaid. The further collection of taxes seemed impossible; the assessments were in hopeless confusion. War was going on in the East, on the Rhine, and in Italy, and civil war, in La Vendée. All the armies had long been unpaid, and the largest loan that could for the moment be effected was for a sum hardly meeting the expenses of the government for a single day. At the first cabinet council Bonaparte was asked what he intended to do. He replied, "I will pay cash or pay nothing." From this time he conducted all his operations on this basis. He arranged the assessments, funded the debt, and made payments in cash; and from this time—during all the campaigns of Marengo, Austerlitz, Jena, Eylau, Friedland, down to the Peace of Tilsit in 1807—there was but one suspension of specie payment, and this only for a few days. When the first great European coalition was formed against the Empire, Napoleon was hard pressed financially, and it was proposed to resort to paper money; but he wrote to his minister, "While I live I will never resort to irredeemable paper." He never did, and France, under this determination, commanded all the gold she needed. When Waterloo came, with the invasion of the Allies, with war on her own soil, with a change of dynasty, and with heavy expenses for war and indemnities, France, on a specie basis, experienced no severe financial distress.

If we glance at the financial history of France during the Franco-Prussian War and the Communist struggle, in which a far more serious pressure was brought upon French finances than our own recent Civil War put upon American finance, and yet with no national stagnation or distress, but with a steady progress in prosperity, we shall see still more clearly the advantage of meeting a financial crisis in an honest and straightforward way, and by methods sanctioned by the world's most costly experience, rather than by yielding to dreamers, theorists, phrase-mongers, declaimers, schemers, speculators or to that sort of "Reform" which is "the last refuge of a scoundrel." *•

There is a lesson in all this which it behooves every thinking man to ponder.

---

*For facts regarding French finance under Napoleon I am indebted to Hon. David A. Wells. For more recent triumphs of financial commonsense in France, see Bonnet's articles, translated by the late George Walker, Esq. For general subject, see Levasseur.

MILLS COLLEGE LIBRARY